From the Editors of The MILEPOST®

ALASKA

A TO Z

A handy reference to the places, people, history, geography and wildlife of Alaska.

Vernon Publications Inc.

Bellevue, Washington

Editor: Kris Valencia Graef
Cover Design: David L. Ranta
Publisher: Geoffrey P. Vernon
Associate Publisher: Michele Andrus Dill
Production Manager: Barton R. Vernon
Fulfillment Manager: Tina L. Boyle
Cover photo: Jason Paur
Cartography: David L. Ranta

Chukchi
Sea

Russia
U.S.

Big Diomede Is.

Kotzebue

Little
Diomede
Is.

Wales

International Dateline

Seward
Peninsula

St.
Lawrence
Island

Nome

Bering Sea

Nunivak
Island

Bethel

Pribilof Islands

Attu Island

Bristol
Bay

Kiska Island

Aleutian Islands

Unimak
Island

Alaska

Adak

Atka

Unalaska

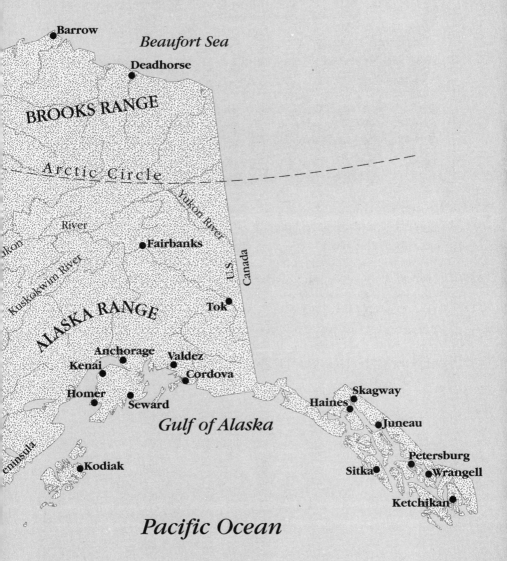

Vernon Publications Inc.
3000 Northup Way, Suite 200
Bellevue, WA 98009-9643
(425) 827-9900 • 1-800-726-4707
Fax (425) 822-9372
E-mail: books@alaskainfo.com
Internet address: www.alaskainfo.com

Arctic Ocean

Barrow

Beaufort Sea

Deadhorse

BROOKS RANGE

Arctic Circle

Yukon River

River

U.S.

Canada

Fairbanks

Kuskokwim River

ALASKA RANGE

Tok

Anchorage

Valdez

Kenai

Cordova

Homer

Seward

Skagway

Haines

Juneau

Gulf of Alaska

Petersburg

Kodiak

Sitka

Wrangell

eninsula

Ketchikan

Pacific Ocean

This Frank Whaley photo of Chester and Helen Seveck was taken in Kotzebue. The Sevecks promoted Alaska for Wien Alaska Airlines throughout the United States and in Japan for some 20 years. They performed traditional Eskimo dances for President Reagan and on the Art Linkletter, Steve Allen and Groucho Marx television shows. They also performed during the early years of the Eskimo-Indian Olympics, which Helen's brother, Howard Rock, helped found in the mid-1960s in Fairbanks. Chester Seveck died at the age of 91 in January 1981. Helen continued her work with the Alaska tourism industry. She passed away at the age of 87 in December of 1993.

• Adak Island

Adak Island is located in the Adreanof Islands group, about midway down the Aleutian Island chain. The southern end of Adak is part of the Alaska Maritime National Wildlife Refuge. The entire 28-mile-long island was a restricted military installation and Alaska's largest naval base until the base closed April 1, 1997. The base has been turned over to private contractors to maintain the facilities.

Though archeological evidence suggests earlier habitation, the island was unoccupied at the outbreak of World War II. In 1942, the military constructed an airstrip at Adak in just 10 days, using steel landing mats. The runway was used by the 11th Army Air Force fighters and bombers operating against Japanese installations on Attu and Kiska islands.

See also *Aleutian Islands, Attu Island, Kiska Island & World War II.*

• Admiralty Island

Admiralty Island is the largest island in southeastern Alaska. It was named by British explorer Capt. George Vancouver in 1794. Tlingit Indians called it Kootznoowoo, "Fortress of Bears." The 96-mile-long island contains the 955,000-acre Admiralty Island National Monument. More than 90 percent of the island is designated wilderness area. Kootznoowoo Wilderness Area has the densest population of brown bears in the world—one per square mile.

Other wildlife includes Sitka blacktail deer, river otters, beavers, harbor seals, whales and sea lions. A large number of bald eagles nest along the coastline near Seymour Canal. Popular recreational activities include canoeing and kayaking, hiking, hunting, fishing, bird watching, nature study and photography.

Just 15 miles from Juneau, Admiralty Island is considered an ideal wilderness laboratory. During World War II, Natives of the Pribilof and Aleutian Islands were relocated here, though most left after the war ended. Today, the Tlingit settlement of Angoon is the only permanent village on Admiralty.

See also *Pack Creek Bear Observatory, Tlingit Indians & Tongass National Forest.*

◆ Afognak Island

The second largest island in the Kodiak archipelago, mountainous Afognak is 50 miles in length and, along with the smaller Raspberry Island, home to Alaska's only herds of elk. A non-native species, the Roosevelt elk were transplanted to the island in the 1920s.

See also *Elk.*

◆ Agattu Island

Agattu Island, the southernmost of the Near Islands in the Aleutian Chain, was called *Ostrov Kruglyy* ("round island") by early Russian fur traders and explorers. The name Agattu is an Aleutian word first reported as "Agataku" by Reverend William Coxe in 1787, and gradually transmuted into Agattu. The water passage between Agattu and Attu islands likewise came to be known as Agattu Strait.

Russian explorer Michael Nevodchikof, who sailed with Vitus Bering, tried to land at Agattu with some crewmen, but they were frightened off by Natives who paddled out to meet them.

See also *Aleutian Islands, Attu Island & Vitus Bering.*

◆ Agriculture

Alaska has a colorful history of farming and agricultural projects—predominantly in the Tanana and Matanuska-Susitna river valleys. Early Russian settlers first tried farming at Kodiak, but lack of training and an unfavorable climate limited their success. The booming population during the Klondike gold rush days led to further development, and during that time the federal government established a series of agricultural experiment stations that developed many new varieties of vegetables and grains hardy enough to withstand the varied, northern climate.

One of the most unusual agricultural experiments in Alaska was the Matanuska Valley Colony. As part of a New Deal plan to aid American farmers hard hit by the Great Depression, and also utilize the agricultural potential of the Matanuska-Susitna valleys, 203 Midwest farm families were transplanted to Palmer in 1935. Although the program was considered a failure, it led to the permanent establishment of farming in the Mat-Su Valley.

Today, Alaska's annual agricultural income ranks among the lowest of the 50 states. But Alaska is famous for its giant vegetables, with cabbages as large as 98 pounds and turnips more than 30 pounds entered at state fairs. Important crops include barley, hay and potatoes. Livestock products, such as milk, eggs and beef, account for almost one-third of the state's farm income.

See also *Delta Barley Project, Matanuska Valley Colony & Palmer.*

◆ Akutan Island

The Russian Navy reported this Aleut name for the island in 1768. Akutan Island is in the Krenitzin Islands, the first group of islands off the Alaska Peninsula in the Aleutian chain. When the Japanese bombed nearby Dutch Harbor on Unalaska Island and occupied Attu and Kiska islands at the end of the Aleutian chain during World War II, Akutan's inhabitants were evacuated to the Ketchikan area. Most of the island's current population, around 400 people, live in Akutan city on the east coast of the island. The island has a 4,275-foot active volcano (Akutan Volcano).

See also *Aleutian Islands, Volcanoes & World War II.*

◆ Alaska

The state of Alaska includes 586,000 square miles—by far the largest state in the union and one-fifth the size of the continental United States. Bordered by two oceans and three seas, Alaska contains 3,000 rivers, 3 million lakes and 5,000 glaciers. Mt. McKinley/Denali is the tallest peak in North America at 20,320 feet.

Known as The Last Frontier, much of Alaska is sparsely populated. Alaska ranks 50th in the United States in population per square mile, with about 1.07 square miles per person. The state's resident population is 550,043.

In 1867, the United States bought Alaska from Russia for $7.2 million—about two cents an acre. On January 3, 1959, Alaska was admitted to the union as the 49th state. The name Alaska is derived from the Aleut word "Alyeska," meaning "great land."

See also *Alaska Purchase, State Symbols & Statehood.*

◆ Alaska Commercial Company

Soon after the U.S. purchase of Alaska in 1867, seven American men met in San Francisco to form the Alaska Commercial Co. in order to buy the assets of the Russian-American Co. Such colorful figures as Francois Mercier and his brother Moise helped the company flourish. In 1901, to meet growing competition and a worsening post-gold-rush economy, it merged with the Seattle-Yukon Co., the Alaska Exploration Co. and the Empire Transportation Co. to form two new firms: the Northern Navigation Co., which would handle river transportation, and the Northern Commercial Co., to operate a mercantile business.

See also *Russian-American Co.*

◆ Alaska Day

Alaska Day, Oct. 18, is an official state holiday marking the anniversary of the formal transfer of Alaska from Russia to the United States, and the first raising of the American flag at Sitka.

See also *Alaska Purchase & Seward's Day.*

◆ Alaska Eskimo Whaling Commission (AEWC)

In 1977, the International Whaling Commission banned all hunting of bowhead whales by Natives and non-Natives, disrupting the traditional Eskimo practice of subsistence hunting. The Eskimos countered with the formation of the Alaska Eskimo Whaling Commission, a self-regulating committee, which allowed them to negotiate limited whale hunting.

See also *Eskimos, Umiak & Whaling.*

◆ Alaska Federation of Natives (AFN)

The Alaska Federation of Natives is a political organization formed by 17 Native organizations in 1966 to pursue settlement of their land claims against the federal government. Almost a hundred years after the U.S. purchase of Alaska from Russia, the AFN represented the first statewide organization offering a unified position on Native land use and occupancy in Alaska.

From 1966 until 1971, the AFN worked to attain passage of a just and fair land settlement, which resulted in the passing of the Alaska Native Claims Settlement Act (ANCSA) in 1971. ANCSA provided the Natives with title to 44 million acres of land and $962.5 million, in return for their relinquishing aboriginal land rights. After the passage of ANCSA, the AFN offered a variety of human services programs and technical assistance to Natives.

Today, the organization's mission includes the goals of advocating Native rights at the federal, state and local levels; encouraging the preservation of Alaska Native cultures; promoting increased understanding of the economic needs of Alaska Natives and protecting and enhancing their lands; and instilling increased pride and confidence in individual Natives.

See also *Alaska Native Brotherhood, Alaska Native Claims Settlement Act, Native Corporations & Natives.*

◆ Alaska Highway (Alcan)

Until the Alaska Highway was built in 1942, waterborne transportation dominated travel to and within Alaska. The idea of an overland link between the Lower 48 and Alaska was investigated as early as 1930, when President Hoover authorized a study of the project; however, the American government didn't begin developing serious plans for such a route until 1940. After the bombing of Pearl Harbor by the Japanese in December 1941, America realized the vulnerability of Alaska to foreign attack.

By February 1942, the United States and Canada had developed a plan to build a highway to Alaska following an existing chain of airfields. In the spring, the Army Corps of Engineers began construction of the pioneer road at Dawson Creek, BC, and after eight months of seven-day-a-week construction, the road was completed, connecting to an existing road to Fairbanks. The Canadian government cooperated in the effort by providing rights-of-way and construction materials, and waiving import duties, sales and income taxes and immigration regulations.

Construction crews faced not only long, strenuous hours, but mosquitoes and black flies in summer and icy temperatures in winter. The project

took on a new sense of urgency after the Japanese occupied the Aleutians in June 1942. By October 1942, the pioneer road was passable to Fairbanks. It was dedicated on November 20, 1942, at Soldiers Summit, YT. In March 1943, the pioneer road was officially named the Alaska Highway, replacing ALCAN, the military acronym for the Alaska-Canada military highway. Civilian travel on the new highway was restricted during the war years for security reasons and after the war because of the lack of services. It wasn't until Feburary 1948, that the Alaska Highway was officially opened for tourists.

The Alaska Highway is open year-round. Paving was completed about 1984, and today the greatest distance between services is only about 75 miles. The Alaska Highway starts at Milepost 0 in Dawson Creek, BC, and extends through Yukon Territory to its official end at Delta Junction, AK, Milepost 1422.

For mile-by-mile information on the Alaska Highway, consult *The MILEPOST®*, the bible of North Country travel since 1949 (Vernon Publications Inc.).

✦ Alaska-Juneau Mine (A-J Mine)

The Alaska-Juneau Mine, one of the most profitable low-grade gold mines in Alaska, operated from 1897 until 1944. The ruins of the old A-J mill may be seen on a hillside above Gastineau Channel just south of Juneau. The A-J Mine produced $80 million in gold before it was declared a nonessential wartime activity and closed by the government in April 1944.

See also *Gold, Juneau & Mining.*

✦ Alaska Marine Highway

Ferry transportation to and within Alaska is provided by the Alaska Marine Highway, which is the name of the state ferry system and also refers to the water route the ferries follow from Bellingham, WA, to Skagway, AK. There are two Alaska state ferry systems, Inside Passage/Southeast and Southcentral/Southwest. They do not connect with one another. State ferry service was inaugurated in May 1963, between Prince Rupert, BC, and Southeast Alaska.

The Southeast system serves 7 mainline ports (Ketchikan, Wrangell, Petersburg, Sitka, Juneau/Auke Bay, Haines and Skagway) from Bellingham, WA, and Prince Rupert, BC. It is a three day trip between Bellingham and Skagway. The Southcentral system serves Cordova, Valdez, Whittier, Seward, Homer, Seldovia, Kodiak, Port Lions, Chignik, Sand Point, King Cove, Cold Bay, False Pass and Unalaska.

All Alaska state ferries carry both vehicles and passengers, but not all ferries have cabins. The ferries are named for Alaska glaciers: *Aurora*, *Columbia, LeConte, Malaspina, Matanuska, Taku, Bartlett* and *Tustumena*.

For more information, contact the Alaska Marine Highway (see For More Information section) and consult *The MILEPOST®* (Vernon Publications Inc.).

✦ Alaska National Interest Lands Conservation Act

In 1980, President Jimmy Carter signed the Alaska National Interest Lands Conservation Act (ANILCA), which set aside close to 103 million acres as national parks, wildlife refuges, wilderness areas and wild and scenic rivers. Also known as the Alaska Lands Act, it was prompted by a provision in the 1971 Alaska Native Claims Settlement Act that required the government to set aside more "national interest" lands in Alaska.

See also *Alaska Native Claims Settlement Act & National Parklands.*

✦ Alaska Native Brotherhood

A forerunner to the Alaska Federation of Natives, the Alaska Native Brotherhood (ANB) was founded in 1912 by Southeast Alaska Natives. The main purpose of the organization was to win citizenship and defend Native land rights. The ANB helped push through a 1915 territorial act allowing Natives to become citizens, although most Natives did not become cititzens until the U.S. Citizenship Act of 1924.

◆ Alaska Native Claims Settlement Act (ANCSA)

The Alaska Natives' claim to the land of Alaska was recognized by the U.S. Congress as early as 1884, but the issue of ownership remained unsettled until 1968, when the North Slope oil strike prompted immediate settlement. Native land claims stood in the way of a pipeline construction permit, and the support of oil companies for a definitive settlement finally ensured the speedy passage of a land claims act.

With the Alaska Native Claims Settlement Act, the Natives relinquished aboriginal claim to their lands on December 18, 1971; in return they received title to 44 million acres of land and were paid $962.5 million. The land and money were divided among 13 regional, four urban and more than 200 village Native corporations organized by ANCSA. Those eligible to enroll in the corporations included any Alaska Natives born on or before the date of the settlement who could prove one-quarter Native ancestry.

The act was amended on Feb. 3, 1988, providing further protections to undeveloped Native corporation lands, the right for shareholders to issue stock to Natives not originally enrolled and to children born after the deadline, and for shareholders to make other changes in the Native corporation structure.

See also *Alaska Federation of Natives, Native Corporations & Tyonek.*

◆ Alaska Peninsula

The Alaska Peninsula juts out 550 miles from mainland Alaska, from Iliamna Lake to the Aleutian Islands. To the northwest are Bristol Bay and the Bering Sea, to the southeast Shelikof Strait and the Pacific Ocean. In 1778, Capt. James Cook was the first to correctly apply the Native name "Alaschka" to the land.

Katmai National Park and Preserve, Aniakchak National Monument and Preserve and the Alaska Peninsula National Wildlife Refuge are all located on the peninsula. The peninsula features active volcanoes, such as Pavlof and Veniaminof; Naknek and Becharof lakes; and the Alagnak, Egegik and Naknek river systems. Towns on the Alaska Peninsula include Chignik, Cold Bay and King Cove.

See also *Aniakchak National Monument and Preserve, Katmai National Park and Preserve, Becharof Lake, McNeil River & Volcanoes.*

✦ Alaska Permanent Fund

In 1976, the people of Alaska voted to create the Alaska Permanent Fund; 25 percent of all mineral lease proceeds received by the state are deposited into the fund. Income from the fund is then put to three uses: annual dividends paid to every resident who applies and qualifies; funds added to the principal account to compensate for inflation; and remaining income appropriated by the Legislature for various uses.

The fund was established to benefit present and future Alaskans by investing a portion of the income derived from development of the state's non-renewable resources, primarily petroleum. The Permanent Fund has established itself as one of the largest pools of public money in the United States; it's one of the top lenders to the U.S. government among all American funds. It is projected that by the year 2000 the fund will be producing more revenues for the state than Prudhoe Bay.

See also *Oil & Prudhoe Bay.*

✦ Alaska Purchase

By the mid-1800s, the once-prosperous Russian-American Co. was losing money. Its main source of revenue—the fur seal—was only beginning to recover from overhunting. Russia decided it no longer wanted to support the company, or keep the land of Alaska. At the same time, President Abraham Lincoln's Secretary of State, William Henry Seward, was advocating stronger U.S. control over the North Pacific and North Atlantic by purchasing Alaska from Russia, and Greenland and Iceland from Denmark.

In 1859, Baron Edouard de Stoeckl of Russia traveled to the United States from St. Petersburg with the authority to sell Alaska. The United States was interested, but the Civil War interrupted negotiations. In 1866, talks resumed, and Seward, now under President Andrew Johnson, actively pursued the acquisition. DeStoeckl had originally been authorized to sell the land for $5 million, but Seward, in his desire to obtain Alaska, too hastily raised his bid and de Stoeckl was able to garner $7.2 million from the transaction.

The Treaty of Purchase was signed at four o'clock in the morning on March 30, 1867, by Seward and de Stoeckl. On a rainy day in Sitka, Oct. 18, the Russian flag was lowered and the American flag (with 37 stars) was raised. After the transfer, only a few Russians remained in Sitka. Many Americans, believing Alaska to be a wasteland of ice and snow, referred to it as Seward's Folly, or Seward's Icebox.

See also *Alaska Day, William Henry Seward & Seward's Day.*

◆ Alaska Railroad

The Alaska Railroad operates year-round passenger and freight service. Its main line extends 470 miles from Seward to Fairbanks. Construction of the railroad began in 1915 under President Woodrow Wilson. On July 15, 1923, President Warren G. Harding drove in the golden spike at Nenana, celebrating completion of the railroad. The railroad was federally owned and operated until January 1985, when the state of Alaska purchased the line and rolling stock.

During summer, rail service is available daily along the 350-mile railway line between Anchorage and Fairbanks (12-hour train ride), with a stop at Denali National Park. Summer service is also available between Anchorage and Seward (115 miles, 4 1/2 hours); and between Anchorage and Whittier (2 1/2 hours), or between Portage and Whittier (35 minutes), via the 12.4-mile Whittier Cutoff. This spur line was constructed in 1942-43 as a safeguard for the flow of military supplies. Rail service is greatly reduced in winter. For further information, contact the Alaska Railroad Corp. (address and phone in For More Information section).

◆ Alaska Range

The Alaska Range extends in an arc across southcentral Alaska, from Iliamna Lake in the southwest to White River in the southeast. The 650-mile range contains Mt. McKinley/Denali (the highest point in North America at 20,320 feet) and Mt. Foraker (17,400 feet). Drained by the Yukon and Kuskokwim rivers, the northern slopes are the main watershed between the Pacific Ocean and the Bering Sea. The Alaska Range is the most inland section of the Pacific Mountain System.

See also *Mt. McKinley/Denali & Mountains.*

◆ Alaska Road Commission (ARC)

The Alaska Road Commission was established in 1905, the same year the first automobile arrived in Alaska at Skagway. The ARC operated for 51 years, building roads, airfields, trails and other transportation facilities. It was replaced by the Bureau of Public Roads (referred to by many Alaskans at the time as the Bureau of Parallel Ruts) in 1956. In 1960 the Bureau of Public Roads was replaced by the Department of Public Works.

See also *Highways.*

◆ Alaska Syndicate

Financiers J.P. Morgan and Simon Guggenheim began investing in Alaska copper and coal mines at the turn of the century. Together their interests came to be known as the Guggenheim-Morgan, or Alaska, Syndicate. In 1908, Guggenheim-Morgan bought out the largest shipping company serving the North and formed the Alaskan Steamship Co.

A controversy arose that same year when the Alaska Syndicate began building a railroad from Cordova to the Chitina and Copper river valleys. A rival businessman decided to start a railroad in Valdez. When the construction crews crossed paths in Keystone Canyon, shots were fired. Public opinion over the incident leaned strongly against the syndicate. The subsequent trial was fraught with bribery and coercion, and ended with a single conviction for assault with a deadly weapon.

See also *Cordova & Railroads.*

◆ Alaskaland Pioneer Park

Built in Fairbanks in 1967, this Alaska Centennial Park commemorates the 100th year of American sovereignty over Alaska. The 44-acre park offers a flavor of interior Alaska history. Exhibits include Gold Rush Town, an authentic street of downtown Fairbanks buildings from its early 20th-century gold rush era; the Pioneers of Alaska Museum; the Native Village Museum and Kashims, with Native crafts and artifacts; Mining Valley, with displays of mining equipment; the Pioneer Aviation Museum; the Crooked Creek & Whiskey Island Railroad; and a visitor center aboard the sternwheeler *Nenana.* For further information, contact the Fairbanks Convention and Visitors Bureau (address and phone in For More Information section).

◆ Alcan

See *Alaska Highway.*

◆ Alcohol

The legal drinking age is 21. The possession and/or the sale of alcoholic beverages is prohibited in some 70 bush communities.

◆ Aleutian Islands

Williwaws—strong, blustery winds—characterize the Aleutian Islands, also renowned for their thick fogs and sudden squalls. The islands arc off the Alaska Peninsula, and are the partially submerged extension of the Aleutian Range of mountains. Known as the Aleutian chain, or just "the Chain," the Aleutians include 14 large islands, 55 small islands and numerous islets. Adm. Adam Johann von Krusenstern first used the name Aleutian (already applied to the islands' Natives) in 1827 to refer to the chain.

The islands are divided into five groups: the Andreanof Islands, the Fox Islands, the Islands of the Four Mountains, the Near Islands and the Rat Islands. They form a natural divider between the Bering Sea and the Pacific Ocean.

See also *Aleuts; Adak, Agattu, Akutan, Amchitka, Attu, Atka, Kiska and Unimak islands; Islands, Unalaska & World War II.*

✦ Aleutian Range

The Aleutian Range, an extension of the Alaska Range, stretches 600 miles along the southeast side of the Alaska Peninsula, and continues under the sea. The peaks of these submerged mountains form the Aleutian chain. The range unites with the smaller Chigmit mountains at the southwest point of Cook Inlet. It has many active volcanoes, including Novarupta in Katmai National Park and Preserve, which erupted in 1912, and Mount Redoubt, which erupted in 1989.

See also *Katmai National Park and Preserve & Volcanoes.*

✦ Aleuts

The Aleuts are the indigenous people of the Aleutian Islands. They are related to the Eskimo people in terms of race and ethnicity, but have their own language and culture. Traditionally, the Aleuts subsist on sea lions, seals, whales and fish. They are also famed for their excellent basketry.

Prior to the arrival of the Europeans, an estimated 20,000 Aleuts inhabited the island chain. In the 1700s, the arrival of the Russians, who sought fur seals and sea otters, brought the healthy Aleut culture to a tragic halt. The Natives were forced to work for the Russians, and a majority of the adult population was killed as a means of terrorizing the survivors into submission.

In 1942, after the Japanese bombed Unalaska and Dutch Harbor, all Aleuts residing west of Unimak Island and from the Pribilof Islands were evacuated to Southeast. Many never returned. When the Japanese occupied the islands of Attu and Kiska, they interned a number of the islands' residents in Japan, where many perished. The internment and relocation further devastated the Aleut communities. Today, only 8,000 Aleuts remain.

See also *Aleutian Islands, Anangula, Barabara, Basketry, Bidarka, Carving and Sculpture, Natives, Whaling & World War II.*

◆ Alexander Archipelago

The 1,100 islands of the Alexander Archipelago, the peaks of a submerged section of the Coast Range, lie off the southeastern coast of Alaska. Divided by deep fjords, the islands protect the Inside Passage (a water route along Alaska's panhandle) from strong weather patterns. Prince of Wales is the largest island of the group; other major islands include Baranof, Chichagof, Kupreanof and Admiralty. Most Southeast communities are located on islands in the archipelago.

See also *Admiralty Island, Chichagof Island & Prince of Wales Island.*

◆ Alyeska

An Aleut word meaning "the great land," Alyeska was first used to refer to the Alaska Peninsula and later to the entire state. The name now is most commonly used to refer to the popular ski resort on Mt. Alyeska, a 3,939-foot peak in the Chugach Mountains just outside Anchorage.

◆ Amchitka Island

Amchitka Island, 35 miles long and 3 miles wide, is one of the Rat Islands in the Aleutian chain. It gained attention during World War II, when the United States military built an air base there, and again from 1965 to 1973, as the site of underground nuclear testing by the Atomic Energy Commission. In 1988, a U.S. Navy radar station was built on Amchitka because of the island's location: It is closer to the former Soviet Union than it is to any U.S. city. However, the base shut down in September 1993, a casualty of the end of the Cold War.

See also *Aleutian Islands.*

◆ Anaktuvuk Pass

This Nunamiut Eskimo village, in Anaktuvuk Pass along a historic caribou migration route, is the last remaining settlement of the inland northern Inupiat Eskimo, whose ancestors date to 500 B.C. The original nomadic

Nunamiut bands left the Brooks Range and scattered in the early 1900s, but by 1938 several Nunamiut families began returning to the mountains at Killik River and Chandler Lake to settle permanently at "the place of caribou droppings." This North Slope village is located within the Gates of the Arctic National Park and Preserve.

See also *Eskimos & Gates of the Arctic National Park and Preserve.*

◆ Anan Bear Observatory

Managed by the U.S. Forest Service, Anan Bear Observatory is 35 miles southeast of Wrangell and accessible only by boat or plane. During July, August and mid-September bears congregate to feed on spawning pink salmon. The only facilities are a concrete observation building and a public-use recreation cabin. Tours are available from Wrangell. For further information contact the Forest Service Information Center (address and phone in For More Information section).

See also *Bears & Pack Creek Bear Observatory.*

◆ Anangula

Dating back an estimated 8,000 years, Anangula is the oldest known Aleut settlement. This site is located on now-uninhabited Anangula Island at the northern end of Samalga Pass near Nikolski village. Stone artifacts have been found at Anangula linking this culture to those of northern and central Asia. The site appears to have been occupied for less than a century when a heavy cover of volcanic ash from Okmok Volcano probably killed local plants and animals on which the people depended. The 4,000-year gap between the early settlement and later evidence of human habitation in the area appears to correspond to a period of volcanic activity.

See also *Aleuts & Archeology.*

◆ Anchorage

Anchorage, Alaska's largest city with a population of 226,338, is on Knik Arm in Cook Inlet. In many ways Anchorage is a typical urban setting, and its international airport is known as the "Air Crossroads of the World." However, the sight of a moose in a suburban backyard is not uncommon, and the edges of wilderness are minutes away.

Anchorage is surrounded by dense forests of spruce, birch and aspen, and the Cook Inlet branches of Turnagain and Knik arms. The Chugach

Mountains rise over the city from the east. Anchorage's climate resembles that of the Rocky Mountains; the average temperature in January is 13°F, while in July it's 58°, and snowfall averages 70 inches per year.

Established as the construction camp and headquarters of the Alaska Railroad in 1913, the town gained its name from Knik Anchorage, just offshore of the site. Other early names included "Ship Creek" and "Woodrow." In 1964, the city was heavily damaged by an earthquake. Millions of dollars of government relief funds were spent on rebuilding.

Alaska Pacific University, the University of Alaska at Anchorage, Elmendorf Air Force Base and Fort Richardson are all in the greater Anchorage area. The city has a number of tourist attractions and is the site of the annual Fur Rendezvous.

See also *Alaska Railroad, Anchorage Fur Rendezvous, Aviation, Chugach Mountains, Cook Inlet, Good Friday Earthquake, Military Bases, Museums, Skiing & Universities and Colleges.*

◆ Anchorage Fur Rendezvous

Commonly known as "Rondy," the Anchorage Fur Rendezvous is a major event each February. It began as a fur auction in 1934, with buyers coming from many parts of the world to purchase pelts from Alaska trappers, but the festivities today center around arts and crafts exhibits, a costume ball, a traditional Native blanket toss and the World Championship Sled Dog Race. For further information, contact the Anchorage Visitor Information Center (address and phone in For More Information section).

◆ Aniakchak National Monument and Preserve

The main feature of this 600,000-acre park, located on the Alaska Peninsula 10 miles east of Port Heiden, is the Aniakchak Caldera. The 6-mile-wide, 2,000-foot-deep caldera was created some 3,500 years ago by the collapse of a 7,000-foot volcano. The caldera was officially discovered in 1922 by a government geologist. Another interesting feature of the caldera is a 2,000-foot-deep canyon, called "The Gates," which has eroded through the caldera's rim. The Aniakchak River flows through The Gates, emptying into the Pacific Ocean at Aniakchak Bay.

Established in 1980, Aniakchak is one of Alaska's most remote national parks. Wildlife includes brown bears, caribou, eagles and red salmon. Common activities are hiking and camping, fishing, natural history study, rafting and beach-walking.

See also *National Parklands.*

◆ Anvil Creek

More than one creek in Alaska bears this name, but the most famous Anvil Creek is near Nome, site of the first mined gold in the Nome district and the Alaska gold rush of 1900, which followed the famous Klondike gold rush of 1897-98. Unlike the Klondike, Anvil Creek and other gold-rich areas near Nome were accessible directly by ship from Seattle.

See also *Nome & Gold.*

◆ Archeology

Many archeological studies in Alaska focus on Beringia—the area that the Bering Land Bridge covered. Archeologists have excavated a number of sites throughout the state, trying to uncover the details of the migration of people to the New World during the last Ice Age. The Dry Creek site near Healy shows evidence of occupation as long as 11,000 years ago. Some scientists estimate people migrated to Alaska as long as 30,000 years ago. Other significant discoveries include sites at Onion Portage, Cape Krusenstern and Anangula.

See also *Anangula, Barrow (Birnirk), Bering Land Bridge National Park (Trail Creek Caves), Cape Denbigh, Cape Krusenstern National Monument, Dinosaurs, Fossils, Kobuk Valley National Park (Onion Portage) & Point Hope (Ipuitat).*

◆ Arctic Circle

The Arctic Circle is the latitude at which the sun never sets on the day of the summer solstice (June 20 or 21) and never rises on the day of the winter solstice (December 21 or 22). For about two months during summer, the sun shines continually; during winter there are two months of darkness. The only light is that of the moon and the aurora borealis (northern lights).

The northern third of Alaska lies within the Arctic Circle—the only true polar region in the state. The Brooks Range separates the Arctic region from the Interior of Alaska and, surprisingly, the temperature in the Interior is often more severe, as the Arctic Ocean has an ameliorating effect on temperatures in the Far North.

See also *Aurora Borealis, Climate, Daylight Hours & Regions.*

✦ Arctic National Wildlife Refuge

The 19.3-million-acre Arctic National Wildlife Refuge (ANWR), located in the northeast corner of Alaska, is the most northern of Alaska's wildlife refuges. Designed to preserve the migration routes of the Porcupine caribou herd, ANWR is also home to musk oxen, Dall sheep, wolverines, polar and grizzly bears, wolves, moose and about 140 bird species. Heightened interest in ANWR in recent years has been attributed to the continuing debate over development of natural resources, especially oil, in the region.

✦ Arts and Crafts

 Authentic Alaskan arts and crafts are fashioned by either Native (Eskimo, Aleut, Indian) or non-Native resident Alaskans using indigenous or imported materials. Materials indigenous to Alaska include gold nugggets, ivory, jade and soapstone (also imported), hematite, Alaska coral, fish skin leather, moose and caribou hides and antlers, wild animal furs, baleen, musk ox wool, birch bark, red and yellow cedar, tree fungus, dried flowers and beach grasses. The state has a voluntary licensing program to help identify authentic Native crafts (Silver Hand symbol) and non-Native made in Alaska crafts (Bear symbol).

Alaskan arts and crafts embrace a number of art forms. Carvings of animals and various other shapes in ivory, soapstone, jade, horn and antler are found in many gift shops and museum stores.

Masks, models (bidarkas and other miniatures) and baskets in the Eskimo, Indian and Aleut tradition are popular Native Alaskan crafts.

Dolls have a long history in Alaska Native culture and are in great demand. Primarily an Eskimo craft, dolls were made for children but often had their roots in the shamanic tradition.

Athabascan beadwork is available in the form of earrings, bracelets, necklaces, eyeglass cases and medicine bags.

Other Alaska arts and crafts include art prints, paintings, painted gold pans, gold nugget jewelry, wood carvings, musk ox wool (qiviut) knitted hats, knitted dog fur hats, parkas, kuspuks, ceremonial blankets and ulus.

See also *Basketry, Beadwork, Carving and Sculpture, Chilkat Blankets, Diamond Willow, Ivory, Masks, Totem Poles & Ulus.*

◆ Athabascans

Members of North America's largest linguistic family, the Alaskan Athabascans are relatives of the Navajos and Apaches of the American Southwest. The Athabascans inhabited most of interior Alaska before the influx of Russians and Europeans. Their existence was semi-nomadic and extremely difficult. Following the seasonal movements of fish and game along the rivers of the Interior, they faced long periods of famine and extremes in temperature.

There are seven subgroups of Alaskan Athabascans: Ahtna (Ahtena), Eyak, Ingalik (Tena), Koyukon, Kutchin, Tanaina and Tanana. Only two of these groups, the coastal Tanaina and the Eyak, reside along salt water.

See also *Beadwork, Languages, Natives, Nulato Massacre & Skin Sewing.*

◆ Atka Island

Six months after the Japanese attack on Pearl Harbor, rugged, volcanic Atka Island—largest of the Andreanof group in the Aleutian Chain— was bombed by the Japanese. Residents were evacuated to the Ketchikan area. After the war, residents were returned to Atka, along with residents of Attu Island, which the government decided was too remote for re-settlement.

The village of Atka is the westernmost and most isolated Native village in the Aleutian chain. The island has been occupied for at least 2,000 years. Native women of Atka, and also Attu, are famous for their grass (wild rye) basketry skills.

See also *Aleutian Islands, Aleuts, Attu Island, Basketry & World War II.*

◆ Attu Island

Attu and Kiska islands—seized and occupied by the Japanese during 1942—are the only American lands to be occupied by a foreign country since the War of 1812. The attack was used to divert the attention of U.S. forces from other World War II battlegrounds. A schoolteacher who tried to send out news of the invasion was killed, and all the other inhabitants were interned in Japan. Only about half of them survived.

In May 1943, U.S. troops defeated the Japanese at Massacre Bay on the island, but only after a bloody, 19-day battle in which nearly 5,000 U.S. and Japanese troops were killed or wounded. The United States government decided Attu, the westernmost island in the Aleutian chain, was too remote to rebuild, and the Attuans were instead sent to Atka Island.

Massacre Bay had earned its name from an earlier tragedy on the island. In the late 18th century, Russian fur-seekers murdered all the Aleut males from the village of Attu on the shore of this bay after a dispute arose over the Aleut women.

The entire island is part of Alaska Maritime National Wildlife Refuge. In 1981, a memorial was dedicated to honor the American soldiers who fought and died there.

See also *Aleutian Islands, Aleuts, Atka Island & World War II*

◆ Aurora Borealis (Northern Lights)

The aurora borealis, or northern lights, range from simple arcs to drapery-like forms in green, red, blue and purple. In northern latitudes, such as Alaska, auroras most often occur in the spring and fall months because of the tilt of the planet in relation to the sun's plane. But displays may occur on dark nights throughout the winter.

The auroras are a natural phenomenon caused by the presence of charged particles in the earth's magnetic field. Electrons and protons released through sun spot activity emanate into space; a few drift to Earth where the planet's magnetic forces pull them to the most northern and southern latitudes.

"We've got to stop considering Alaska as merely an outpost and consider it an integral part of the United States. More than that, we've got to recognize it as a key to continental defense."

— Congressman Warren G. Magnuson, 1941

19

◆ Aviation

Because of the sheer size of Alaska, the lack of roads and the remoteness of many of its villages, air travel has historically been an important and popular form of transportation. Alaska boasts an amazing six times as many private pilots per capita and 16 times as many private aircraft per capita as the rest of the United States. There is one pilot and one aircraft for every 61 Alaskans. Alaskan private pilots average more than 100 hours flying time annually, compared with the 43 hour average per pilot for the rest of the U.S. Alaska also ranks first in number of floatplane bases (102). Lake Hood in Anchorage is the largest and busiest floatplane base in the world.

Commercial aviation in Alaska began in Fairbanks in 1923, when Carl Eielson flew the first scheduled mail flight between Fairbanks and McGrath. Air travel quickly became the dominant form of transportation in Alaska. Eielson later formed his own airlines, as did many other bush pilots who pioneered air travel in Alaska during the 1920s and 1930s. Starting with one or two planes, these early airlines chartered themselves out to carry passengers, mail, furs and anything else that would pay the freight. Dozens of start-up companies failed, or merged with other airlines. Today, about 10 domestic airlines and two dozen small scheduled carriers serve Alaska

Alaska Airlines, the largest and one of the oldest domestic airlines in Alaska, grew to prominence by acquiring or merging with eight other airlines. Its parent company—McGee Airways, formed in 1932 by Linious "Mac" McGee—provided service between Anchorage and Bristol Bay in a single-engine, three passenger plane. Alaska Airlines currently is the tenth-largest airline in the U.S. and serves cities along the West Coast and Hawaii from Alaska. Reeve Aleutian Airways, another pioneering regional airline founded in 1932, continues to be owned and operated by the Reeve family. Reeve serves the Aleutian Islands, St. Paul in the Pribilofs, Russia and Hawaii.

See also *The Bush, Carl Ben Eielson, the Norge, Northwest Staging Route & Noel Wien.*

◆ Baleen

Baleen—a fringed plate of elastic, horny material—lines the mouths of baleen whales and filters out fish and krill during feeding. In the past, the black, bony plates were used by Europeans and Americans to make buggy whips and corset stays. Today, some coastal Natives use baleen for handcrafted items.

See also *Whales & Whaling.*

◆ Banana Belt

The Alaska "banana belt" refers somewhat facetiously to the milder climate in the southcentral and southeast coastal areas. Winters in the banana belt are relatively warmer than in the frigid interior region; warmed by Pacific currents, the area gets more rain than snow, and temperatures rarely drop too far below zero.

◆ Barabara

Influenced by traditional Aleut dwellings, which were communal, partially underground structures, barabaras are smaller, semi-subterranean houses built of wood and sod. They post-date the Russian-occupied period in Alaska history and were common in the Aleutian chain. Though now outmoded, the structures were excellent at keeping the warmth in and the cold out. Occupants entered through holes in the roof and used notched logs for stairs.

✦ Alexander Baranof

Alexander Baranof (1747-1819) was chief manager of the Russian-American Co. and the first governor of Russian Alaska. Baranof took over management of Shelikof's Russian colony on Kodiak Island in 1790. In 1799, when the Russian government consolidated the various trading companies into the Russian-American Co., Baranof moved the Russian-American capital to Sitka. He arrived in Sitka Sound in July, purchased a tract of land from the local Tlingit chief, and built Redoubt Saint Archangel Michael about 7 miles north of present-day Sitka.

In 1802, local Tlingits destroyed the fort. In 1804, Baranof returned with a Russian warship and bombarded the Native encampment. Baranof then built New Archangel on the site of present-day Sitka.

The Tlingit name "Sitka," meaning "best place," soon predominated over Baranof's New Archangel. Sitka became the capital city of Russian Alaska in August 1808, and ships from California, the Sandwich (Hawaiian) Islands, Siberia and China called at its harbor.

U.F. Lisianski, a Russian captain, named the 105-mile island on which Sitka is located after Baranof.

See also *Kodiak Island, Russian-American Co., Gregorii Shelikof, Sitka & Tlingit Indians.*

✦ E.T. Barnette

Elbridge Truman Barnette, born in Akron, Ohio, in 1863, came north with the gold rush in 1897, and is credited with founding Fairbanks.

See also *Fairbanks.*

✦ Barrow

Barrow (pop. 3,469), on the coast of the Chukchi Sea, is the government seat of the North Slope Borough, the world's largest municipal government in terms of area. Barrow takes its name from Point Barrow, which was named in 1826 by Capt. Beechey for Sir John Barrow, secretary of the British Admiralty and patron of Arctic exploration. Its traditional name is *Ukpeagvik,* "place where owls are hunted."

When oil was discovered in 1968 on the North Slope—just 200 miles east—the town boomed. By the time the trans-Alaska pipeline was completed, the boom was over, but Barrow had become a modern community in the process.

Barrow is one of the largest Eskimo communities in the world. Whaling is central to the Eskimo culture here, and tourism is the community's major industry. Barrow's "top of the world" location has made it a popular tourist destination since 1954, when Wien Alaska Airlines initiated air tours to Barrow. Historic sites in Barrow include Utkeagvik Presbyterian Church and the Will Rogers and Wiley Post monument across from the airport. (There is also a monument at the crash site, about 12 miles southwest of Barrow and not accessible by road.) Archeological sites at Birnirk (500-900 A.D.) near Barrow include the Utkeaviq Site, where a frozen family was unearthed from Mound 44 in 1982. Cape Smythe Whaling and Trading Station in nearby Browerville is the oldest frame building in the Arctic, built in 1893.

See also *Eskimos, North Slope, Oil, Prudhoe Bay, Whaling & Will Rogers and Wiley Post Monument.*

◆ E.L. "Bob" Bartlett

Bob Bartlett, territorial delegate to U.S. Congress from 1944-58, became one of the first Alaska state senators after the territory achieved statehood in 1959, serving until his death in 1968. As a delegate, he was instrumental in fighting for statehood; in 1966 his Fur Seal Act granted local government powers to Aleuts.

See also *Statehood.*

◆ Basketry

The Aleut people produce some of the most renowned and highly prized baskets in Alaska. Made from rye grass, the most common form of Aleut basket is a small, cylindrical shape with a knobbed lid. The three main styles of Aleut baskets are named after their islands of origin—Attu, Atka and Unalaska. The fine weave was traditionally decorated with spruce roots, feathers, caribou hair and colored grass. After the arrival of Europeans, the Aleuts also began to use silk threads and worsted wool.

The Inupiat Eskimos of northern Alaska produce baleen and birch bark baskets. The baleen basket, traditionally made by men, is the only Native basket made exclusively for trade. The craft was suggested by a whaling company trader named Charles D. Brower in the early 1900s. Baleen baskets are typically finished with an ivory top piece, furnished by an ivory carver. Baskets woven of beach grasses using a coil technique are a craft of the Yup'ik Eskimos of southwestern Alaska. The durable and functional Athabascan baskets are made of birch bark or willow root.

See also *Aleuts, Athabascans & Natives.*

◆ Beadwork

Beadwork is most often representative of the Athabascan Indian culture of Interior Alsaka. Clothes and belongings of the semi-nomadic Athabascan Indians living in this harsh climate were made of tanned hides and furs of local animals, and often adorned with beads of carved wood, seeds, quills and shells. Glass trade beads, introduced in the mid-nineteenth century by Europeans, were also incorporated into the beadwork. Intricate beadwork motifs of flowers, leaves and berries are found on mittens, moccasins and other items of clothing and jewelry.

See also *Athabascans, Eskimos & Skin Sewing.*

◆ Bear Paws

Bear paws are stubby, rounded snowshoes commonly used for traveling short distances on hilly terrain.

◆ Bears

Alaska is home to black bears, brown/grizzly bears and polar bears. Black bears range throughout most of the state, with the highest densities in Southeast, Prince William Sound and Southcentral. They are omnivores, favoring berries and salmon. Black bears can be brown or cinnamon in color; another rare, Alaska color variation is the "glacier" or "blue" bear, which has a smoky blue or gray coat. Black bears may be confused with grizzly/brown bears, although they are normally smaller (125 to 400 pounds), with a more pointed head.

Brown bears have a distinct shoulder hump and larger head than black bears. The coat of a brown bear may vary from black to blond, and they range over most of the state. The McNeil River, in particular, has a great concentration of brown bears.

Brown and grizzly bears were once thought to be different animals. Research has proven, however, that they are indeed the same bear species, having adapted to different habitats. Interior brown bears (grizzlies) have a lean, protein-poor diet and live in a much harsher climate than the larger, coastal brown bears, which thrive in the milder climate and salmon-rich country. Alaska's coastal brown bears are the world's largest carnivorous land mammal.

Polar bears are larger than brown bears, but they live at sea on the Arctic ice pack. They have a heavy white coat, tinged with yellow, a long neck and small head. Polar bears are strong swimmers and their main food source is the ringed seal, though they also eat walrus, birds, fish and some vegetation. They have hollow hairs which collect heat, helping them withstand the frigid Arctic weather.

See also *Anan Bear Observatory, Katmai National Park and Preserve, McNeil River & Pack Creek Bear Observatory.*

◆ Beaufort Sea

The Beaufort Sea, part of the southern Arctic Ocean, is located on the northern coast of Alaska, and the northwest coast of Canada. In 1826, English explorer Sir John Franklin named the sea for his friend, Sir Francis Beaufort, a hydrographer to the British Admiralty. Today, the Beaufort Sea is the site of offshore oil leases north of Prudhoe Bay.

See also *Oil & Prudhoe Bay.*

◆ Beavers

Beavers are found throughout most of mainland Alaska from the Interior to the Alaska Peninsula and Southeast. They also have been successfully introduced to Kodiak and its surrounding islands.

Beaver feed on the leaves, roots and bark of a variety of trees, including aspen, willow, birch and cottonwood. Their dams profoundly change the environment, creating large ponds that can stabilize watersheds, reduce flooding and raise water tables. Some fish species benefit from beaver ponds, but salmon runs are sometimes destroyed by the beavers' construction habits.

Russian fur hunters valued beaver furs second only to sea otters. They were hunted almost to extinction by 1910, but hunting bans between then and 1921 allowed the species to recover. Today, limits are set annually.

◆ Becharof Lake

The second-largest lake in Alaska, 37-mile-long Becharof Lake is located on the Alaska Peninsula in the 1.2-million-acre Becharof National Wildlife Refuge. Surrounded by low hills and tundra wetlands to the northwest and volcanic peaks to the southeast, the lake covers a quarter of the refuge. The islands in Becharof Lake are home to many brown bears, due to the number of salmon spawning streams feeding the area. In 1868, the lake was named by William H. Dall of the U.S. Coast and Geodetic Survey for a navigator of the Imperial Russian Navy who was at Kodiak in 1788.

See also *Lakes*.

◆ Vitus Bering

Vitus Bering (1681-1741) is credited with discovering Alaska for Russia. In 1725, Peter the Great of Russia placed Bering, a young Danish sailor, in command of an expedition to find out if the continents of Asia and America were connected and to claim new lands for Russia.

On his first voyage, after traveling over 6,000 miles of land and sailing from the Kamchatka Peninsula, Bering sighted two islands on St. Diomede's Day (Aug. 16) 1728, and named them for the saint. Although in sighting distance of America while sailing through the strait that now bears his name, heavy fog shrouded the land from Bering and his crew. They returned to Russia, and the expedition was considered a failure.

In 1741, on Bering's second expedition, he sighted and named Mt. St. Elias. During a storm, his two ships—the second one under the command of Alexei Chirikof of the Russian Imperial Navy—became separated. According to ship logs, Chirikof sighted Alaska's southeast coast on July 15; he sent three scouting parties to shore, but none returned. (Tlingit legend tells of white men dressed in bearskins, who were ambushed by warriors.) Chirikof and the rest of his men returned to Russia. Bering sighted land

(Kayak Island) on July 16; onshore, his scouts found little food and saw no people. Bering continued his voyage.

By September, Bering's crew was suffering from scurvy and other forms of malnutrition. Turning back to Russia, they encountered a violent storm and were shipwrecked on what is now called Bering Island. A diet of sea otters cured many of the men, but half of them, including Bering, died. The remaining crew built a ship from the wreckage of the *St. Peter* and returned to Russia with a load of otter pelts.

Despite the ravages Bering and his men had suffered, high prices received for the pelts prompted others to return. In 1783, the first permanent Russian settlement was established at Kodiak Island.

See also *Alexander Baranof, Bering Land Bridge National Park, Bering Sea and Bering Strait, Diomede Islands, Kayak Island, Otters & Georg Wilhelm Steller.*

◆ Bering Glacier

The 125-mile-long Bering Glacier, on the southeast coastline between Yakutat and Cordova, is the longest glacier in Alaska. It is second only to Malaspina Glacier in total mass and heads in the enormous Bagley Icefield. The glacier was named in 1880 by the U.S. Coast and Geodetic Survey to commemorate Russian Capt. Cmdr. Vitus Bering, who first set foot in Alaska in this area in July 1741.

See also *Vitus Bering & Glaciers.*

◆ Bering Land Bridge National Preserve

The 2.8-million-acre Bering Land Bridge National Preserve—named for Danish explorer Vitus Bering—marks the remains of the land bridge that connected Asia and North America between 14,000 and 25,000 years ago. The park, established in 1980, is located just below the Arctic Circle, 50 miles south of Kotzebue and 90 miles north of Nome.

During the glacial epoch, as oceans rose and fell, the land bridge between the two continents periodically formed a migratory route for people, plants and animals; this area is also referred to as Beringia. The bridge widened to 1,000 miles at times, and is covered now by the Bering and Chukchi seas. An archeological site at the Trail Creek caves shows evidence of human habitation dating back 10,000 years.

Today, Eskimos continue to pursue a subsistence lifestyle and manage reindeer herds in the area. Wildlife includes more than 110 migratory bird species; seals, walrus, and whales; grizzly bears, wolves, caribou, moose and musk oxen. Recreational opportunities include hiking, camping, fishing, sightseeing and wildlife observation.

See also *Archeology, Vitus Bering & National Parklands.*

◆ Bering Sea and Bering Strait

The Bering Sea, named in 1822 by Russian Capt. V.M. Golovnin for Danish explorer Vitus Bering (who discovered Alaska for Russia), lies between Siberia and Alaska in the northern Pacific Ocean. The 55-mile-wide Bering Strait connects the Bering Sea with the Arctic Ocean to the north. It also separates the continents of Asia and North America. The strait was named in 1778 by British Capt. James Cook.

See also *Vitus Bering & Chukchi Sea.*

◆ Berries

Alaska has more than 50 species of wild berries representing 15 different families. Largest is the Rose family, with 18 species including the popular raspberry, salmonberry, wild and beach strawberries, and the prickly wild rose hips. Second largest is the Heath family with 12 species, including the popular and useful lowbush cranberry and the tasty Alaska blueberry. The Saxifrage family includes the sought-after northern red currant, used in jams and jellies. Poisonous species are the honeysuckle and red elderberry, 2 of the 4 species in the Honeysuckle family, and the deadly baneberry in the Crowfoot family. Rounding out the berry family list—with both edible and inedible species—are the Cypress, Lily, Sandalwood, Goosefoot, Oleaster, Ginseng and Dogwood.

◆ Bethel

Bethel, one of western Alaska's largest communities (pop. 4,674), is on the banks of Kuskokwim River in the Yukon-Kuskokwim Delta. Moravian missionaries established a mission there in 1889. The name Bethel is drawn from the Biblical passage Genesis 35:1, which states, "Arise, go up to Bethel, and dwell there." Today, the Bethel economy is largely based on the commercial fishing industry. Bethel is located within the largest national wildlife refuge in the United States—the 20-million-acre Yukon Delta National Wildlife Refuge.

◆ Bicycling

Road conditions in Alaska vary from newly paved highways to unimproved dirt roads. Cyclists must sometimes contend with steep grades, the absence of shoulders and traffic. One advantage to summer touring is long daylight hours, especially in the month of June. Alaska is suited for all types of bicycle riding, from leisurely to long distance or rugged trail-riding. A variety of maps and guidebooks are available, and private companies offer guided tours. For further information, contact the Alaska Division of Tourism (address and phone in For More Information section).

◆ Bidarka

A bidarka is an Aleut skin boat. Usually a one-man craft, bidarkas are similar in shape to an Eskimo kayak. Aleuts used them for transportation and to hunt seals, sea lions and whales.

See also *Kayak & Umiak.*

◆ Billiken

A Kansas City woman patented the billiken in the early 1900s; however, this grinning, pointy-headed, good luck charm is now manufactured for sale to the tourist trade in Alaska. The billiken bears no relationship to Alaska Native heritage.

◆ Birds

More than 400 bird species have been recorded in Alaska, 174 of which are permanent residents. Birds from five continents migrate here; each summer there are more birds in Alaska waters than in the entire Lower 48.

The Pribilof and Aleutian islands are the site of great seabird colonies, with kittiwakes, murres, auklets, puffins and fulmars. Other important waterfowl nesting areas and migration sites include the Yukon Flats and Yukon-Kuskokwim Delta; the Innoko, Chickaloon, Susitna and Stikine flats; Port Moller; and Izembek Bay.

One of the top attractions for bird watchers is the bald eagle, which is prevalent throughout Southeast. Bird enthusiasts can spot many other unique species throughout the state, such as the trumpeter swan, peregrine falcon and several species of raptors. Some popular bird-watching sights are Potter Marsh and the Westchester Lagoon and Coastal Trail in the Anchorage area, and the Copper River Delta near Cordova. Alaska has five chapters of the Audubon Society, located in Anchorage, Juneau, Fairbanks, Kasilof and

Kodiak. For further information, contact the Anchorage Audubon Society (address and phone in For More Information section).

See also *Camp Robber, Eagles & Puffins.*

◆ Bison

After disappearing from the state of Alaska more than 500 years ago, the American bison was reintroduced in 1928. Twenty-three animals from Montana were brought to the Delta Junction area, and large herds have since developed. As grazers, their numbers are naturally limited by Alaska's climate and terrain. A bull may weigh more than 2,000 pounds; cows are about half that size. This massive bovine is characterized by its shaggy hair and large shoulder hump.

See also *Delta Barley Project.*

◆ Blanket Toss

The blanket toss, or *Nalukatak*, is a traditional Eskimo game involving a circle of people holding a walrus skin stretched taut. A person standing in the middle of the skin is tossed higher and higher into the air, until he/she fails to land on his/her feet. Often, the origin of the game is attributed to an Eskimo tradition of lofting hunters into the air to spot game more easily across the flat tundra and frozen ocean.

Actually, Nalukatak originated as a woman's game, performed during spring whaling festivals. If the wife of a whaling captain had given birth to a son that year, she would stuff candies in her pockets, and they would fly out to the crowd as she was bounced into the air. Today, the blanket toss is often included in Native and community events, such as the Anchorage Fur Rendezvous and World Eskimo-Indian Olympics.

See also *Anchorage Fur Rendezvous, Eskimos & World Eskimo-Indian Olympics.*

◆ Blubber

Blubber, the fat of whales, walrus and seals, is used as a source of food, lubricant and lighting fuel by Natives in many coastal areas of Alaska.

See also *Muktuk.*

◆ Boating, Canoeing, Kayaking and Rafting

Alaska offers thousands of miles of challenging and scenic waterways for sailboats, cruisers, canoes, inflatable rafts or kayaks in its coastal waters and inland rivers and lakes. Southeast offers sheltered transportation routes and recreational opportunities in the Inside Passage and Prince William Sound. Numerous marine charter services are available throughout southeastern and southcentral Alaska, most offering sportfishing and sightseeing tours. Sea kayakers, who are drawn from around the world to Alaska's protected waterways and challenging coastline, can visit tidewater glaciers and natural hot springs.

Inland boaters will find hundreds of river and lake systems suitable for travel by boat, raft, kayak or canoe. Float trips for all skill levels can be arranged in most areas of the state; there are canoe trails near Fairbanks and Anchorage, and on the Kenai Peninsula and Admiralty Island. Alaska's rivers are rated by the International Scale of River Difficulty (from the calm waters of Class I to the nearly impossible navigability of Class VI).

For further information, consult *The ALASKA WILDERNESS GUIDE*, available from Vernon Publications, and contact the Bureau of Land Management, the Alaska Division of Tourism and the Alaska Public Lands Information Center (addresses and phone numbers in For More Information section).

See also *Bidarka, Kayak, Rivers & Umiak.*

◆ Boomers

Alaska's many economic booms—from furs to gold, salmon and oil—have brought waves of new or temporary residents to the state. Boomers come for the sole purpose of getting rich quick off Alaska's natural resources. Prior to the establishment of the state Permanent Fund, the "boom and bust" cycle was an economic norm in Alaska.

See also *Fishing, Gold, Oil & Promyshlenniki.*

◆ Bore Tide

Bore tides, occurring regularly in Cook Inlet at Turnagain and Knik arms, are fast-moving walls of water capable of reaching 6 feet in height. Caused by a surging tide moving into a narrow estuary, bore tides are steep, foaming and often dangerous waves.

✦ Boroughs

Unlike the rest of the United States, which is organized into counties, Alaska's unit of regional government is the borough, and each borough has independent, incorporated communities within its boundaries. Alaska currently has 16 organized boroughs, with the rest of the state essentially unorganized. Ranked by population (largest to smallest) the boroughs are: Anchorage, Fairbanks North Star, Matanuska-Susitna, Kenai Peninsula, Juneau, Ketchikan Gateway, Kodiak Island, Sitka, North Slope, Northwest Arctic, Haines, Aleutians East, Lake and Peninsula, Denali, Bristol Bay and Yakutat.

✦ Breakup

Breakup is that time in spring when frozen rivers break up and significant amounts of ice and snow melt within a short period. Signaling the end of winter and the beginning of summer, breakup often means flooding rivers, pot-holed streets and plenty of mud.

See also *Nenana Ice Classic.*

✦ Bristol Bay

Bristol Bay, one of the richest fisheries in Alaska, is 270 miles wide at the mouth, which stretches from Cape Newenham on the north to the Alaska Peninsula and Unimak Island on the south. Capt. James Cook named the bay in 1778 in honor of Adm. Earl of Bristol, England.

See also *Canneries & Fishing.*

✦ Brooks Range

The Brooks Range, extending east from Canada to the Chukchi Sea on the west, forms the water divide between Arctic Slope drainage to the north and the Kobuk and Yukon rivers to the south. It also divides the broad, coastal plain of the North Slope in the Arctic region from the Interior. The Brooks Range includes nine different groups of mountains, with peaks ranging in height from 4,000-9,000 feet. Some of the tallest peaks are Mt. Isto (9,058 feet), Mt. Chamberlin (9,019 feet) and Mt. Michelson (8,855 feet).

The range was named in 1925 for Alfred Hulse Brooks (1871-1924), the chief Alaskan geologist of the Geological Survey from 1903 to 1924.

See also *Gates of the Arctic National Park and Preserve, Mountaineering, Mountains, North Slope, Taiga & Tundra.*

◆ Buffalo

See *Bison*.

◆ Bunny Boots

Bunny boots, also known as vapor barrier boots, are white, insulated footwear designed to protect feet in sub-zero temperatures. They take their name from the Arctic hare, which has large hind feet and a white winter coat.

◆ The Bush

Originally used to describe large expanses of wilderness inhabited by trappers and miners, now "the Bush" is generally considered to mean any part of Alaska inaccessible by road. A community accessible only by air, water, sled or snow machine transportation is considered a bush village. The Bush is home to many of Alaska's Native people and to many Alaskans who live on homesteads, operate mines or work as guides, pilots, trappers or fishermen.

The term "bush" has been applied to the small planes and their pilots who service areas that lack roads or developed airports. Bush planes are commonly equipped with floats or skis, depending on the terrain and season.

See also *Aviation, Carl Ben Eielson, Population, Subsistence & Noel Wien.*

William A. Wallace Collection

✦ Cabin Fever

Cabin fever is a malady said to be caused by too much darkness and cold, and cramped quarters. It is common in mid-winter Alaska when the sun is absent and springtime a faraway cure. Humorist Tom Bodett says, "You know you've got it if you've been having homicidal fantasies about your dog at night because you can hear it breathing."

✦ Cabins

A number of wilderness cabins are available for public use in Alaska. The Forest Service manages more than 200 cabins located throughout the Tongass and Chugach national forests; they are accessible by boat, air or trail. The Bureau of Land Management also has cabins, most of which are located in the White Mountains National Recreation area, north of Fairbanks. In Kodiak National Wildlife Refuge, the U.S. Fish & Wildlife Service manages cabins, and Alaska State Parks has both remote and road-accessible public-use cabins scattered throughout the state.

The cabins vary in size and amenities. Most have tables, benches, bunks, a stove (wood or oil) and pit toilets. Most cabins must be reserved well in advance; special drawings are held for some during high-use periods. Fees range from $20 to $50 per night depending upon location. Prices are subject to change. For further information, contact the Alaska Public Lands Information Center (address and phone in For More Information section).

✦ Cache

A cache is a small cabin on stilts used in the Bush to store food and belongings safely from animals.

✦ Camp Robber

Also known as the Canada Jay or Whiskey Jack, Camp Robber is the all-too-suitable name for the gray jay. These bold birds with insatiable appetites will help themselves to almost anything edible they can carry away.

See also *Birds*.

✦ Camping

Established campgrounds are maintained by a variety of federal and state agencies in Alaska, along with private enterprise. With few exceptions, government and private campgrounds are located along the road system. Wilderness camping is also available in most state and federal parklands.

Federal agencies offering recreational campsites in Alaska are the Bureau of Land Management (BLM), the National Park Service, the U.S. Forest Service and the U.S. Fish and Wildlife Service. BLM, which oversees approximately 90 million acres of federal land in Alaska, maintains 11 campgrounds, most located in Interior Alaska. The U.S. Forest Service operates 26 established campgrounds on some 22.7 million acres of national forest land in Alaska. The 17-million-acre Tongass National Forest, the largest national forest in the U.S., has 11 campgrounds. Chugach National Forest—the second largest national forest in the U.S. with 5.6 million acres—has 15 campgrounds. Of Alaska's 15 national parks, preserves and monuments, only three have established campgrounds: Denali National Park and Preserve (7 campgrounds), Glacier Bay National Park and Preserve (1) and Katmai National Park and Preserve (1). The U.S. Fish & Wildlife Service manages several campgrounds within Kenai National Wildlife Refuge, and offers wilderness camping on other refuge lands in Alaska.

Alaska State Parks, the largest state park system in the United States with more than 3 million acres of land, maintains more than 3,000 campsites within its 120-unit park system. Camping is available at 40 state recreation sites, 5 state parks (Chugach, Denali, Chilkat, Kachemak Bay and Wood-Tikchik), 14 state recreation sites and a state historic park.

For further information, consult *The MILEPOST®* and *The ALASKA WILDERNESS GUIDE*, both available from Vernon Publications, or contact Alaska State Parks, the Bureau of Land Management, the Alaska Public

Lands Information Center and the Alaska Campground Owner's Association (see For More Information section).

◆ Canneries

Americans began preserving salmon in tin cans in the late 1800s. Alaska's first salmon cannery was established at Klawock on Prince of Wales Island in 1878. Canneries are located near fisheries throughout Southeast, Southcentral, Southwest and western Alaska. All five species of Pacific salmon are canned: king salmon, labeled "chinook"; coho (silver) salmon, labeled "medium red"; pink (humpback), labeled "pink"; and chum and sockeye, marketed as chum and sockeye. Crab and shrimp are also canned.

At the height of the fishing season, seasonal workers may be brought in from outside. Canneries may stay open around the clock to meet the incoming fish, and fisherman are given limits when the canneries have reached capacity. Canning has been the dominant method of preserving salmon, although improved freezing methods and air transportation have added other markets.

See also *Fishing, King Cove, Naknek & Salmon.*

◆ Cape Denbigh

A point of land at the east end of Norton Sound, facing the Bering Sea, Cape Denbigh was named in 1778 by Capt. Cook. There are two archeological sites on Cape Denbigh, Nukleet and Iyatayet. Iyatayet, on the east shore of Cape Denbigh, was a momentous discovery and is a national historic landmark. It was older than any previously known site and contained evidence of the Arctic small tool tradition. Located on an old beach ridge, Iyatayet was excavated by archeologist J.L. Giddings from 1948-52 and represents three cultural periods dating back as far as 5,000 B.P. ("before present," or 1958, the advent and milestone of carbon dating).

See also *Archeology.*

◆ Cape Krusenstern National Monument

Some of the most important prehistoric sites in the Arctic are located in the Cape Krusenstern National Monument. The 660,000-acre monument on Kotzebue Sound contains archeological records of Eskimo communities from every known cultural period in Alaska.

The unique beachscape contains 114 lateral ridges formed by ocean currents, shifting ice and waves. As geological forces formed these ridges, each one was used in succession as an Eskimo hunting camp.

Today, Eskimos continue to hunt seals along the cape's outermost beach. Common activities in the monument include hiking and camping, fishing, sightseeing, wildlife observation and photography. Wildlife includes seals, walrus and whales; 112 species of migratory birds; brown bear, moose, red and arctic foxes, weasels and wolverines; and occasional wolves, caribou and musk oxen. Salmon, grayling and arctic char are found in monument waters.

See also *Archeology, Eskimos & National Parklands.*

◆ Caribou

The Barren Ground caribou—the only deer in which both sexes grow antlers—is found throughout most of Alaska. Constantly roaming to find food, the caribou favors willow, birch, grasses, sedges and lichen. The bull's antlers may be as large as 4 feet from base to tip. The caribou has wide hooves, enabling it to cross snow, ice and slippery gravel slopes with relative ease, and to swim, using the hooves as paddles.

◆ Carving and Sculpture

The Haida, Tlingit and Tsimshian Indians of southeastern Alaska create art in the Northwest Coast tradition. Southeast Natives usually worked with wood, such as cedar. Totem poles are one of the more popularly recognized examples of their carving. Other common items include bentwood boxes and chests, wooden masks and carved rattles.

Natives of the Seward Peninsula and islands of the Bering Sea, renowned for their finely carved ivory figurines, continue a 2,000-year heritage of Eskimo ivory carving. Driftwood is traditionally used to carve bowls, ladles, trays and ceremonial masks. Stone and whalebone are used for larger works.

The Aleuts worked with wood, ivory, stone and bone to make tools, weapons and ceremonial objects. Prior to European contact, most carvings were made for functional purposes. In the 19th century, the emphasis changed to works of commercial value, such as figurines and game boards. However, in contemporary Aleut art, sculptures made of whalebone, wood and stone continue to convey aspects of Aleut culture.

See also *Masks, Ivory & Totem Poles.*

"In this year of our Lord 1898, men are flying northward like geese in the springtime. That not more than one of us has ever set eyes on a real, live nugget passes for nothing; we shall naturally recognize "the yellow" when we see it. It is our intention to ransack Mother Nature's storehouses, provided we can unlock or pry open the doors without losing our fingers by freezing."

— Joseph Grinnell

◆ Cheechako

A cheechako is a newcomer, greenhorn or tenderfoot, and the opposite of a sourdough or oldtimer. The word originated from Chinook jargon, a trade language that combined English and Indian dialects.

◆ Chichagof Island

Chichagof Island lies just north of Baranof Island in the Alexander Archipelago. The 72-mile-long island was named in 1805 by Capt. U.F. Lisianski. Communities include Pelican, Hoonah and Tenakee Springs.

◆ Chicken

Chicken (pop. 37), located on the Taylor Highway, was a mining camp established in 1903. The town was named by the miners, who wanted to call their camp ptarmigan (after the wild bird that roamed freely in the area) but were unable to spell it and settled for the bird's common name—chicken.

◆ Chilkat Blankets

Chilkat blankets—ceremonial blankets made by Alaska's Tlingit Indians—are traditionally woven from mountain goat wool and cedar bark. The beautiful weavings are complemented by hereditary crest, or totemic, designs. Often these designs are the same as those painted on Tlingit house posts.

Pattern boards—smooth cedar boards designed by male artists—are used as guides for the dyed color designs. In the past, these dyes were obtained from a variety of sources, including hemlock bark, urine, moss, iron and indigo blue from European trade cloths.

Chilkat blankets are a status symbol worn on ceremonial occasions, a mark of pride for both the owner and the weaver. Today, these woven dancing blankets are also a popular collector's item.

See also *Tlingit Indians*.

◆ Chilkoot Trail

The Chilkoot Trail was the shortest and best-known route to the Klondike gold fields during the gold rush of 1897-98. The 21-mile trail began at Dyea and peaked at the 3,739-foot summit. Thousands of prospectors climbed the treacherous path, many making the trip more than 20 times to carry their supplies to the other side. White Pass Trail, with a 2,900-foot summit, provided an alternate route, but most of the hurried gold-seekers chose the shorter Chilkoot Trail. Once over the summit, the stampeders built boats at Lake Bennett and followed the Yukon River to the Klondike gold fields.

Today, a few thousand people hike the historic trail every summer. Highlights include The Scales, a former weighing place for packed goods, and The Golden Stairs, a 45-degree climb from The Scales to the summit. During winter, gold-seekers chopped steps into the snow. In summer, the route crosses large boulders.

The town of Dyea, at the start of the trail, once rivaled Skagway as the largest town in Alaska. Today hardly a trace remains of the Dyea townsite, although visitors can still see the remains of Dyea's 1.3-mile-long wharf and Slide Cemetery, where about 60 victims of an 1898 avalanche lay buried.

See also *Gold, Klondike Gold Rush National Historical Park & Skagway.*

◆ Chugach Mountains

The Chugach Mountains extend from Anchorage almost to the Canadian border. Along with the Alaska Range, the mountains surround the city of Anchorage, protecting it from the Interior's frigid winter temperatures (the city's marine location also influences its weather patterns). The Chugach Range converges with the Wrangell and St. Elias ranges in Wrangell-St. Elias National Park and Preserve, forming a vast, rugged wilderness area. Many of Alaska's major glaciers, such as Columbia, Portage, Matanuska and Worthington, head in the Chugach Mountains.

See also *Chugach National Forest, Columbia Glacier, Glaciers, Matanuska Glacier, Mountains & Portage Glacier.*

◆ Chugach National Forest

The Chugach National Forest covers 5.8 million acres east from the Kenai Peninsula, across Prince William Sound to Bering Glacier, encompassing the Copper River Delta and Gulf Coast. The forest is second in size only to the Tongass National Forest in Southeast.

Highlights include Kayak Island, site of the first documented landing of Europeans in Alaska; Columbia Glacier; the Copper River Delta wetlands; the Begich, Boggs Visitor Center (one of the most popular in the state) at Portage Glacier; and a rich variety of wildlife.

More than 214 species of birds reside in or migrate through the Chugach National Forest. Some of these are the black-legged kittiwake, bald eagle and trumpeter swan. Record-size moose inhabit the Kenai Peninsula area. Offshore are marine mammals such as the Dall porpoise, killer and humpback whales, sea otters, sea lions and harbor seals. Saltwater fish include five species of salmon, red snapper and halibut.

The park offers a wide range of recreational opportunities, including a variety of water sports, skiing, snow machining and hiking. For further information, consult *The ALASKA WILDERNESS GUIDE*, available from Vernon Publications, or contact the Chugach National Forest (address and phone in For More Information section).

See also *Columbia Glacier, Kayak Island, Portage Glacier & Tongass National Forest.*

◆ Chukchi Sea

The Chukchi Sea, off Alaska's northwest coast, lies between Alaska and Siberia. Kotzebue Sound faces into this segment of the Arctic Ocean. Bering Strait connects the Chukchi Sea with the Bering Sea.

✦ Circle City

Prior to the Klondike gold rush of 1897-98, Circle City was the largest gold mining town on the Yukon River. Prospectors discovered gold on Birch Creek in 1893. They named the town after the Arctic Circle, in which they erroneously thought it was located. Today, the small community of Circle City lies at the entrance of the Yukon-Charley Rivers National Preserve, and summer river traffic brings increased activity. A local attraction is the old Pioneer Cemetery, with markers dating back to the 1800s.

See also *Gold & Yukon-Charley Rivers National Preserve.*

✦ Citizenship Act of 1924

On June 2, 1924, all the Natives of Alaska—Aleuts, Eskimos and Indians—were made U.S. citizens. As part of the Citizenship Act, the Natives requested medical care, education and land compensation. However, the act brought little aid from the federal government, and Natives did not see further compensation until the passage of the Alaska Native Claims Settlement Act in 1971.

See also *Alaska Native Claims Settlement Act & Natives.*

✦ Clam Gulch

Clam Gulch, on the Kenai Peninsula, is famous for the hundreds of thousands of razor clams harvested annually from its sandy beaches. Clamming there is best at low tides of minus 2 feet or less.

See also *Kenai Peninsula.*

✦ Climate

Alaska's climate varies greatly by region. Southeast (Alaska's panhandle), protected by mountains and warmed by Pacific Ocean currents, has the mildest temperatures and the most rain.

In Southwest, the Aleutian Islands are windy, with frequent squalls and rainstorms, and are notoriously foggy. Shemya Island in the Aleutian Chain has the state's strongest recorded winds, measured at 139 mph. Farther north, on the Bering Sea coast, temperatures are colder than in Southwest, while strong winds and gray skies remain prevalent.

The Interior has the driest climate and most extreme temperatures in the state. Alaska's highest recorded temperature (100°F) occurred at Fort Yukon in June 1915; the coldest temperature (-80°F) was recorded at

Prospect Creek on January 23, 1971. Southcentral is shielded from these frigid temperatures by the Alaska and Chugach mountain ranges, and the Pacific Ocean has an ameliorating affect.

The harshest weather in the state, and perhaps in the world, occurs in Alaska's Arctic region. During winter, the sun doesn't rise for more than two months; snow and ice cover the ground for eight months of the year, while precipitation levels are desert-like.

See also *Arctic Circle, Banana Belt, Daylight Hours, Ice Fog, Regions & Sea Ice.*

◆ Coast Mountains

The Coast Mountains extend 1,000 miles along the mainland portion of Southeast at the Alaska-Canada border. The Coast Mountains are sometimes incorrectly referred to as the Coast Range, which in fact is the name applied to the continuation of the coastal mountain ranges of California, Oregon, Washington and British Columbia. The Coast Range is represented in Alaska by Kodiak Island, the Kenai, Chugach and St. Elias ranges and the islands of the Alexander Archipelago.

See also *Mountains.*

◆ Coastline

Alaska has 6,640 miles of coastline—more than the rest of the U.S. combined. About 5,580 miles of this are along the Pacific Ocean and 1,060 miles are along the Arctic Ocean.

◆ Cold Bay

Cold Bay (pop. 148), 40 miles from the western tip of the Alaska Peninsula, is gateway to the 320,893-acre Izembek National Wildlife Refuge and the 3.5-million-acre Alaska Peninsula National Wildlife Refuge. The area is near the southern edge of the former Bering Land Bridge, and appears to have been inhabited by Asiatic people migrating to North America. The region was given the name Izembek in 1827 by Russian Count Feodor Lutke, when he named the lagoon after his ship's surgeon, Karl Izembek.

During World War II, a large air base was built at Cold Bay. Today, the airport provides a communication and transportation hub for the Aleutian and Pribilof islands.

◆ Coldfoot

Touted as the northernmost truck stop in the U.S., Coldfoot provides a rest stop on one of the most difficult highways in Alaska. Coldfoot is 60 miles north of the Arctic Circle on the Dalton Highway, and has recorded temperatures of -70°F.

Originally called Slate Creek, Coldfoot reportedly received its current name in 1900, when a gold discovery on the Koyukuk River brought prospectors to the area. The stampeders made it to this point before the rugged Interior weather gave them "cold feet," and they turned back. In recent years the town has been rejuvenated as the halfway point on the Dalton Highway (also known as the North Slope Haul Road), between Prudhoe Bay and Fairbanks.

See also *Highways, Prudhoe Bay & Trans-Alaska Pipeline.*

◆ Columbia Glacier

Columbia Glacier on Prince William Sound is one of Alaska's most magnificent tidewater glaciers. Located in the Chugach National Forest, the glacier was named in 1899 by the Harriman Alaska Expedition for Columbia University in New York City.

The glacier is more than 40 miles long with a tidewater terminus of more than 6 miles. Having receded almost a mile in recent years, Columbia Glacier is expected to retreat about 22 miles in the next 20 to 50 years, carving a deep fjord as it recedes. Visible from Columbia Bay, it varies in height from 164 to 262 feet above sea level, and reaches as much as 2,300 feet below the water's surface. Plankton at the face of the glacier attract a number of fish, which in turn draw bald eagles, kittiwakes, gulls and harbor seals.

Columbia Glacier is a major tourist attraction and supports a number of tour boats in Valdez. The state ferry route between Valdez and Whittier also passes within sight of the glacier.

See also *Glaciers & Harriman Alaska Expedition.*

◆ Captain James Cook

Capt. James Cook (1728-79) sailed to America's northwest coast as a commander in the British Royal Navy. Under instructions to determine if the Northwest Passage (a route from the Pacific to the Atlantic) existed, Cook sailed from Plymouth around the Cape of Good Hope to Nootka Sound at Vancouver Island, Canada.

Arriving March 30, 1778, he sailed further north and west as far as Icy Cape in the Arctic Ocean. Cook had sketches made of the previously undefined coastline and named various geographic features. Having failed to locate the Northwest Passage, his ships left Alaska in October 1778 and returned to Hawaii, where Cook was killed by Natives on Feb. 14, 1779.

After his death, the expedition continued to explore the northwest coast, but returned to England a year later, having failed to fulfill its primary mission. The expedition did, however, provide a plethora of information on previously uncharted waters. In 1784, the British Navy published an atlas and an account of the voyage.

Geographic features in Alaska bearing Cook's name include Cook Inlet and Mt. Cook.

See also *Cook Inlet & Northwest Passage.*

◆ Cook Inlet

This 30-mile-wide estuary on the Kenai Peninsula extends 220 miles southwest from Anchorage to Shelikof Strait. The inlet was named by the Earl of Sandwich for Capt. James Cook, who explored the region in 1778. The inlet has great tide ranges; these extremes in turn cause bore tides, especially in Turnagain and Knik arms.

See also *Bore Tides.*

◆ Copper River Highway

Construction on the Copper River Highway, which was to connect Cordova with Chitina and the Richardson Highway, began in 1945. Following the abandoned railbed of the Copper River & Northwestern Railway (CRNW), the highway project was abandoned after the Good Friday Earthquake of 1964 severely damaged the railbed and the Million Dollar Bridge, which crosses the Copper River.

The 48 miles of existing highway, from Cordova to the Million Dollar Bridge, have never been maintained and open to public travel. Under Gov. Hickel, roadwork on the proposed link has continued.

See also *Cordova, Good Friday Earthquake & Railroads.*

◆ Cordova

A small fishing community on Orca Inlet in Prince William Sound, Cordova was established in 1906 by Michael J. Heney, the builder of the Copper River & Northwestern Railway. Cordova was chosen as the end of the line for the railway and developed as a shipping port for copper ore mined near Kennicott. The town and railroad prospered until 1938 when the Kennecott Mine closed. Since then, the community has had a fishing-based economy.

In recent years, debates have continued over whether or not the completion of the abandoned Copper River Highway would help or harm the quiet community. Cordova (pop. 2,110) is connected to Valdez by ferry and has scheduled air service to Anchorage and other communities.

See also *Copper River Highway & Kennecott Copper Mine.*

◆ Council

Near the turn of the century, Council was one of Alaska's largest communities. On the left bank of the Niuluk River, Daniel B. Libby and his party founded the town in 1897. Libby had been a member of an 1896 expedition that discovered gold in the area.

During the summers of 1897-99, Council's population was estimated to be as high as 15,000. In 1900, however, the boom town declined as many headed for the newly discovered gold on the beaches of Nome. The town continued to decline until its post office officially closed in 1953. Remnants of gold mining abound—abandoned buildings, mines, dredges and a railroad. The population today is just 15.

See also *Gold.*

◆ Coyotes

The coyote, now a permanent resident in Alaska, was introduced to the state sometime around 1900. These slender, wolf-like animals have a slight build, standing a little under 2 feet high at the shoulder.

The coyote is a true survivor, managing to scavenge for a living in many areas where other animals perish. The coyote's diet is varied, depending on what is available—small animals, fish, berries, bird eggs and carrion. The coyote is not particularly abundant in Alaska, but is found in many areas of the state.

◆ Craig

Craig (pop. 1,260), on the west side of Prince of Wales Island in Southeast, began as a temporary fish camp for the Tlingit and Haida people. In 1907, Craig Millar, with the help of local Natives, built a saltery at nearby Fish Egg Island. By 1911, a permanent saltery, a cold storage facility and a small community had been established. A post office, sawmill and cannery soon followed. In the 1930s some families from the Midwest Dust Bowl relocated here. Today, fishing continues to be the mainstay of Craig's economy.

See also *Fishing*.

◆ Cruise Ships

Cruise ships play a major role in Alaska's tourism industry. From spring to fall, ships depart from Seattle, WA; Vancouver and Prince Rupert, BC; and Juneau and Anchorage to tour Alaska waters. Within Alaska, smaller cruise vessels and charter boats also conduct tours. Popular sightseeing destinations include Columbia Glacier, Glacier Bay, Tracy Arm, Kenai Fjords National Park and Misty Fjords National Monument. For further information, contact the Alaska Division of Tourism (address and phone in For More Information section).

See also *Alaska Marine Highway, Columbia Glacier, Glacier Bay National Park and Preserve, Kenai Fjords National Park, Misty Fjords National Monument & Tracy Arm-Fords Terror Wilderness Area.*

D

◆ Dall Sheep

The only white, wild sheep in the world, Dall sheep are found in all of Alaska's major mountain ranges. Both sexes have golden-colored horns. The ram's horns are heavy and curled; the female's are thinner and straighter. Lambs are born between mid-May and mid-June. Wolves are the sheep's major predator, although harsh winters exact the greatest toll on their survival rate.

Mac's Foto

◆ Dalton Highway

The 414-mile Dalton Highway was built in 1974 as a haul road between the Yukon River and Prudhoe Bay during construction of the Trans-Alaska pipeline, and was originally called the North Slope Haul Road. Formerly a restricted-access road, the all-gravel highway was officially opened to the public in 1994.

◆ Daylight Hours

SUMMER MAXIMUM

Barrow	Fairbanks	Anchorage	Juneau	Ketchikan	Adak
Continuous from May 10 to Aug. 2	21:49 hrs.	19:21 hrs.	18:18 hrs.	17:28 hrs.	16:43 hrs.

Barrow	Fairbanks	Anchorage	Juneau	Ketchikan	Adak
None from Nov. 18 to Jan. 24	3:42 hrs.	5:28 hrs.	6:21 hrs.	7:05 hrs.	7:46 hrs.

◆ Deadhorse

Deadhorse (pop. 24) is at the northern end of the Dalton Highway. It is not a town in the traditional sense, as it was established to support the oil industry at nearby Prudhoe Bay, and virtually all businesses are engaged in oil field or pipeline support activities. Most buildings are pre-fab and built on gravel pads on tundra bog. Deadhorse takes its name from the airport, which was named after the construction company that built it.

◆ Delta Barley Project

In 1978 the state of Alaska organized Delta Agricultural Project I in which it gave away 60,000 acres of land and created 22 farms to encourage development of an agricultural industry in the Delta Junction area. In 1982, Delta Agricultural Project II conveyed 25,000 more acres and created 15 more farms. The project is commonly referred to as the Delta Barley Project, as barley is the major crop grown in the area.

The Delta barley—an excellent feed for cattle, hogs and sheep—also attracts bison from the Delta Bison Sanctuary, located south of the Alaska Highway. Created in 1980, the 90,000-acre refuge is home to about 500 bison.

◆ Delta Junction

Delta Junction (pop. 736), on the banks of the Delta River at the junction of the Alaska and Richardson highways, is the official end of the Alaska Highway. The town, which began as a construction camp on the Richardson Highway in 1919, is a favorite among tourists interested in viewing and photographing the trans-Alaska pipeline. Originally called Buffalo Center because of its proximity to the winter range of bison that were transplanted to the area in 1927, the town's strategic location at the junction of two major highways helps keep the economy going.

See also *Bison.*

◆ Denali National Park

The entrance to 6-million-acre Denali National Park is located 120 miles south of Fairbanks and 237 miles north of Anchorage. Established in 1917 as Mount McKinley National Park, the park was renamed Denali in 1980. The park's central attraction is 20,320-foot Mt. McKinley—the tallest peak in North America. Clouds obscure the mountain about 70 percent of the time.

Other features in the park include Mount Foraker, at 17,400 feet the third highest mountain in Alaska. Muldrow Glacier, the largest glacier on the north side of the Alaska Range, flows 32 miles from near the summit of Mount McKinley.

The park's wildlife is a main attraction for visitors. Thirty-seven species of mammals (including moose, caribou, grizzly bears and Dall sheep) and 155 species of birds are found here. Other activities include mountain climbing, camping and hiking. Organized activites include nature hikes, sled dog demonstrations and campfire programs. Private operators offer flightseeing tours, bus tours and rafting trips.

Access to the park is via a restricted-use 92-mile gravel road from the park entrance to Kantishna. Within the park there are two visitor centers, one hotel and seven campgrounds. Shuttle bus service is available from the park entrance visitor center to Toklat, Eielson Visitor Center and Wonder Lake. Food, gas, lodging, camping and other services are clustered along the highway near the park entrance.

Denali National Park is open year-round, although most services are available only from late May to mid-September.

See also *Mount McKinley & National Parklands.*

◆ Devil's Club

Easy to identify by its prickly green leaves, and hard to forget for hikers who become entangled in it, Devil's Club flourishes in damp habitats throughout Southcentral and Southeast Alaska. This large shrub is armed with spines from the bottom of its stalk to the top of its leaves. The spines break off easily and can become embedded in the skin, where they will fester if left alone.

Though few enjoy encountering the plant, it is widely used for its medicinal qualities. Devil's Club belongs to the ginseng family and Natives traditionally made tea, pastes or poultices from the plant to soothe or cure everything from black eyes to constipation. It was also believed to have magical powers and to bring good luck.

◆ DEW Line

The DEW Line, or Distant Early Warning Line, is a costly defense system created in 1952 to guard the northwestern shore of Alaska from possible attack across the North Pole. As aviation technology advanced, the threat of a long-range air attack over the Arctic increased. In response, the DEW Line, a system of radar scanning stations ringing northern Canada and Alaska, was built to warn of the approach of enemy planes.

The construction brought an invasion of men, ships, materials and equipment to the Arctic. Engineers had to combat icy waterways, permafrost, muskeg and cold temperatures. The DEW Line was completed in one year.

See also *White Alice.*

◆ Diamond Willow

Diamond willow is a popular material used in handcrafted art and souvenir items. The willow—marked by a diamond pattern in contrasting cream and reddish-brown colors—is not a unique species, but rather has been affected by a fungal attack.

◆ Dillingham

When Alexander Baranof, the first governor of the Russian-America Co., established a trading post at the mouth of the Nushagak River in 1818, the area had long been inhabited by Eskimo and Indian peoples. His post was called Alexandovski Redoubt; but by 1837, the community came to be known as Nushagak. In 1904, it was named Dillingham for William Paul Dillingham, governor of Vermont from 1888-90 and U.S. senator from 1903-23. (In 1903, Sen. Dillingham toured Alaska with his Senate subcommittee—the first comprehensive investigation of the territory by a congressional committee; for years after, Dillingham was considered a Senate authority on Alaska.)

Today, Dillingham, with a population of just over 2,000, is an economic and transportation center for the Bristol Bay region (the world's largest producer of red salmon). The first salmon cannery in the Bristol Bay region was constructed there in 1884, and two more were built nearby in the next two years.

See also *Bristol Bay & Canneries.*

◆ Dinosaurs

In 1961, a Shell Oil Co. scientist discovered some unique fossils on the west bank of the Colville River, near the eastern edge of the National Petroleum Reserve on the North Slope. An expedition of scientists returned to explore the area in 1975 and found almost 200 dinosaur bones. The bones, which were 65 to 70 million years old, were from seven different kinds of dinosaurs, from a 40-pound plant-eater to a 100-pound carnivore.

These arctic dinosaurs seem to disprove the theory that dinosaurs became extinct when a comet or asteroid collided with the earth, creating a cloud cover that lowered temperatures enough to kill them off. The Arctic region was slightly warmer, but even farther north, 65 million years ago.

See also *Fossils.*

◆ Diomede Islands

The Diomede Islands in the Bering Strait are separated by only 2.5 miles of water; but they are in the unique position of being in different time zones, different continents and even different hemispheres. Residents of Little Diomede, in the United States, can look out their windows and see Russia's Big Diomede, already in the next day. The International Dateline and international boundary between the United States and the former USSR run between the two islands. Long ago, the Diomedes were probably part of the Bering Land Bridge.

Vitus Bering named the islands in August 1728. At that time, Diomede residents had an advanced culture, with elaborate whale hunting ceremonies. Islanders traveled to both Siberia and Alaska to conduct trade.

However, after World War II, with the start of the Cold War, residents of the two Diomedes were unable to continue their relations. Big Diomede was turned into a Soviet military base; and on one occasion, Natives of Little Diomede who traveled into Soviet waters were taken captive and held as prisoners in Siberia before being returned.

To this day, villagers are extremely cautious about straying out of U.S. waters. The economy on Little Diomede continues to be subsistence-based. The treeless islands have beachless shores and steep sides.

See also *Vitus Bering, Eskimos & Ivory.*

◆ Dixon Entrance

The Dixon Entrance, at the very southern tip of Alaska's panhandle, is a water passage between British Columbia's Queen Charlotte Islands and the Alexander Archipelago in Alaska. The Dixon Entrance marks the international boundary between Alaska and Canada. The border is about two miles north of British Columbia's Dundas Island. The passage was named in 1787 by Sir Joseph Banks for Capt. George Dixon, who had previously visited it.

◆ Dog Mushing

Once used regularly for transportation and hauling in much of Alaska, working dog teams became a less common sight with the advent of the snow machine. But the sled dog has made a comeback in recent years, due to a resurgence of interest in racing and a rekindled appreciation of the reliability of nonmechanical transportation. In addition to working and racing dog teams, many Alaskans keep sled dogs for recreational mushing. And more winter visitors are experiencing the thrill of mushing.

Sled dog racing is Alaska's official state sport, representing the state's rich frontier tradition. Races are held throughout the winter and range from local club meets to world-class championships. Distances vary (from a few miles to a few hundred miles), as do the number of dogs in a team (anywhere from seven to 16 dogs). Racers are not allowed to replace dogs, so most finish with fewer dogs than they started with due to sore muscles, injuries or tender feet.

Long-distance racing (such as the Kuskokwim 300, the Yukon Quest and the Iditarod) pits racers not only against each other but the elements, too. Sheer survival can quickly take precedence over winning. Besides inclement weather, long-distance racers have to contend with moose scares or attacks on the dogs; overflows on frozen rivers; sudden illness among the dogs; straying off the trail; and sheer exhaustion.

From January through March, it is possible to watch any number of world-class sled dog races in Alaska. Some of the races are: the Clark Memorial Sled Dog Race (Soldotna to Hope, January), the Kuskokwim 300 (Bethel to Aniak, January), the Willow Winter Carnival Race (Willow, January), the Alaska State Championship Race (Kenai-Soldotna, February), the Women's World Championship Race (Anchorage, February), the World Championship Sled Dog Race (Anchorage, February), the Yukon Quest International Sled Dog Race (Fairbanks to Whitehorse or vice versa, February), the Alaska Sweepstakes (Nome to Candle and back, March), the Iditarod Trail Sled Dog Race (Anchorage to Nome, March), the Open North American Sled Dog Championship (Fairbanks, March) and the Tok Race of Champions (Tok, March).

The sport of dog mushing in Alaska also has its heroes. Leonhard Seppala, best known for his role in the life-saving diphtheria-serum run to Nome in 1925, is also remembered for the kindness with which he treated his dogs. The Iditarod's Seppala Humanitarian Award is given to the musher who demonstrates the most humane treatment and care of his team. Dr. Roland "Doc" Lombard, a veterinarian from Massachusetts, became the most successful "outsider" ever to compete in Alaska sled-dog racing by winning 26 championship races. Lombard is also credited with revolutionizing the care and feeding of sled dogs. Athabascan Indian George Attla is the all-time winningest musher, despite having contracted tuberculosis as a child which left him with a permanently locked knee joint. Although he never won a major race, Joe Redington Sr. of Knik is one of the best-known names in the sport. Redington, along with Dorothy Page, organized the Iditarod Centennial race in 1967, which became the annual Anchorage to Nome Iditarod Trail race in 1973. Susan Butcher, originally from Massachusetts, has completed 16 Iditarods, always finishing in the top 10, including four wins: 1986, 1987, 1988 and 1990. She is one of the best-known athletes associated with dog mushing and women's sports.

For further information contact the Alaska Dog Mushers Association (address and phone in For More Information section).

See also *Iditarod Trail Sled Dog Race, Knik & Sled Dogs.*

◆ Dolphins and Porpoises

The playful and intelligent dolphin has long been a favorite of Alaskan mariners and tourists. The Pacific white-sided dolphin, found in the North Pacific (including the Gulf of Alaska and Prince William Sound), is capable of jumping high out of the water, and distinguishes itself by turning somersaults in the air. It has a black back with white stripes and gray sides.

Harbor and Dall porpoises are also found in Alaska waters. The harbor porpoise, usually dark brown or gray, is found from the Arctic Ocean south along the Pacific coast. These extremely shy animals never ride the bows of ships; they most commonly keep to themselves in coastal bays and the mouths of large rivers. Dall porpoises have a more striking appearance; when moving swiftly, their black and white markings sometimes cause them to be mistaken for killer whales. They are found in the North Pacific and its adjacent seas, from the Bering Sea southward.

One other species of dolphin—the grampus—is occasionally sighted as far north as Alaska. It is characterized by scarred skin and a V-shaped groove in its head.

◆ D-2 Lands

Section 17(d)(2) of the 1971 Alaska Native Claims Settlement Act (ANCSA) directed the U.S. Secretary of the Interior to set aside "national interest lands" (such as national parks, wildlife refuges, forests and wild and scenic rivers) by Dec. 18, 1978. The D-2 issue, as it was commonly called, was resolved in 1980, with the Alaska National Interest Lands Conservation Act (ANILCA). Lands designated for federal purposes by ANILCA are sometimes still referred to as D-2 Lands.

See also *Alaska Native Claims Settlement Act & Alaska National Interest Lands Conservation Act.*

◆ Dutch Harbor

See *Unalaska.*

◆ Dyea

See *Chilkoot Trail, Klondike Gold Rush National Historical Park & Skagway.*

◆ Eagle

The town of Eagle (pop. 168) is located on the Yukon River at the end of the Taylor Highway. Francois Mercier established the Belle Isle trading post here in 1874. During the 1880s, Eagle became a supply center for area miners and was a designated customs point. The military established Fort Egbert in 1889, and in 1900 Judge Wickersham presided over the Third Judicial District of Alaska from Eagle's courthouse. The community was incorporated in 1901, but the population declined as miners left for gold strikes in Fairbanks and Nome.

Today, Eagle is a popular jumping-off point for Yukon River travelers. Historical sites include the Wickersham Courthouse, Waterfront Customs House and the mule barn and NCO headquarters at Fort Egbert. A monument to explorer Roald Amundsen, showing the Northwest Passage he discovered, commemorates his arrival in Eagle in December 1905 on foot (his ship was stuck in the ice), to telegraph his discovery to the outside world.

See also Judge James Wickersham & Yukon River.

◆ Eagles

Alaska has more bald eagles than all other states combined. Bald eagles are common in Southeast, Southwest and on the coast of Southcentral, and rare in Interior and western Alaska. Adults are marked by the characteristic white head and tail, while young bald eagles may keep a dusky-colored head and tail for as long as four years. These majestic birds are scavengers, surviving mainly on a rich diet of dead and dying fish. Bald eagles prefer coniferous forests, woodlands, rivers, streams, beaches and tidal flats; they nest in old growth trees, or when in treeless areas, on cliffs or the ground.

Each fall near Haines, thousands of bald eagles fly to the Chilkat River valley to feed on spawning salmon, representing the largest known concentration of bald eagles on the continent. In 1982, the Alaska Chilkat Bald Eagle Preserve, a 48,000-acre state park, was formed to protect them. For information on the preserve, contact Alaska State Parks (address and phone in For More Information section).

Alaska is also a prime habitat for the golden eagle. An adult golden eagle is easily mistaken for an immature bald eagle, but can be distinguished by its smaller head, the golden tone on the back of its neck and its fully feathered legs. Golden eagles are most commonly found in the Interior.

Two eagles sighted on rare occasions in Alaska are the white-tailed eagle and Steller's sea eagle—both Asiatic birds.

See also *Admiralty Island & Birds.*

◆ Earthquakes

Every year in Alaska, there are an average of 1,000 earthquakes of 3.5 or more on the Richter scale. Since the turn of the century, 37 quakes measuring 7.25 or greater have been recorded, and during this period 25 percent of all earthquake energy released in the world has been from earthquakes in Alaska. A 1957 quake in the central Aleutians had a magnitude of 9.1, and in 1965, another quake in the western Aleutians measured 8.7. The Yakutat area experienced a quake with a magnitude of 8.0 in July 1958; it caused a serious landslide in Lituya Bay and a gigantic wave reached 1,740 feet up a mountainside, stripping it down to bedrock.

The most memorable earthquake in recent years was the 1964 Good Friday Earthquake. It caused tremendous damage in the Prince William Sound area and created tidal waves as far south as California. Many of these quakes are caused by the underthrusting of the North Pacific plate, which causes seismicity from the Aleutian Chain inward to interior Alaska.

See also *Good Friday Earthquake.*

◆ Education

In the early 1900s, most Alaska schools (both state and mission schools) forbade the use of Native languages. A 1967 bilingual education act permitted for the first time instruction in non-English languages to children in

> *"In the case of Alaska we have one instance where bluster would not win; fighting was not to be thought of; and so we could pay for the stationary icebergs or let them alone. Nor with money easy, was Alaska a bad bargain at two cents an acre. It was indeed cheaper than stealing..."*
>
> — *Hubert Howe Bancroft, History of Alaska*

American public schools. Later legislation required that every school with more than 14 students whose native language was not English have a teacher fluent in that language.

Another unique aspect of Alaska education is the number of students who receive their education through correspondence schooling; 500 to 800 students are enrolled each year. The state's Centralized Correspondence School (CCS) in Juneau has advisory teachers who conduct courses and maintain close contact with students and home teachers. Another alternative form of education is the Mt. Edgecumbe High School in Sitka—a state-operated boarding school for students from rural areas.

See also *Molly Hootch, Sheldon Jackson & Universities and Colleges.*

◆ Carl Ben Eielson

In the winter of 1929-30, Alaska aviation pioneer Carl Ben Eielson and his mechanic, Earl Borland, died in a plane crash while trying to rescue a shipload of furs from the *Nanuk*, a trading ship trapped in the ice off the coast of Siberia. Eielson and Borland disappeared after taking off from Teller. Eight weeks after they were reported missing, the wreckage of their plane was discovered.

The news made international headlines, as Eielson was a world-famous aviator. In 1923 he began the first scheduled flights in Alaska when he contracted with the Post Office Department to fly bi-weekly mail deliveries between Fairbanks and McGrath. In the spring of 1928, Eielson made the first flight across the North Pole with Sir Hubert Wilkins. That same year, Eielson formed the successful Alaskan Airways.

Eielson Air Force Base near Fairbanks is named after him.

See also *Aviation, The Bush, Military Bases & Noel Wien.*

◆ Eielson Air Force Base

See *Military Bases.*

◆ William A. Egan

William A. Egan, of Valdez, was president of the Alaska constitutional convention and the first elected governor of the state of Alaska. Following the Tennessee Plan (a program first used by Tennessee Territory in its quest for statehood), Alaska's Territorial Legislature elected 55 convention delegates to attend a constitutional convention in 1955, of which Egan was elected president. From there, the convention elected two phantom "senators" and a "representative" to go to Washington, D.C., to lobby for statehood. Egan was chosen to be one of the senators; the other was Ernest Gruening.

See also *Ernest Gruening & Statehood.*

◆ Elmendorf Air Force Base

See *Military Bases.*

◆ Endicott Arm

See *Tracy Arm-Fords Terror Wilderness Area.*

◆ Eskimo Ice Cream

Eskimo ice cream is a traditional snack made of whipped seal oil, berries and sugar.

See also *Eskimos.*

◆ Eskimos

Alaska Eskimos fall into two main groups: the northern Inupiat and the western Yup'ik peoples. Both groups traditionally lived in extended family clans that shared a common territory.

The Inupiat Eskimos, whose name means "the people" in the Inupiat language, are native to Alaska's Arctic region. Barrow, an Inupiat village on the North Slope, is the largest present-day Eskimo community in the United States. Traditionally, the whaling season was the most significant event of the year and whaling continues to provide an economic base. Reindeer herding has also provided a means of surviving in a cash economy, as does the sale of Eskimo art. Also, many Eskimos are employed by the government, or in oil-related projects.

The Yukon-Kuskokwim Delta, in Alaska's southwest, is home to more than 20,000 Yup'ik Eskimos—the greatest population of Natives in any Alaska region. Along the coast and inland rivers are 52 Yup'ik villages. Traditionally, Yup'ik Eskimos have subsisted largely on salmon. Shallow seas made it difficult for early explorers to reach this part of Alaska; consequently the Western world was slower to encroach on the Yup'ik people than other Natives. Today, the Yup'ik language remains predominant in many Native communities, though most Eskimos are bilingual, having been taught English in school.

See also *Alaska Eskimo Whaling Commission, Anaktuvuk Pass, Barrow, Bethel, Bettles, Blanket Toss, Cape Krusenstern National Monument, Diomede Islands, Eskimo Ice Cream, Ivory, Kashims, King Island, Kuspuk, Muktuk, Nunivak Island, Parka, Point Hope, Qiviut, St. Lawrence Island, Ulu, Umiak, Wainwright, Wales, Whaling & World Eskimo-Indian Olympics.*

◆ Events

Following is a list of some of Alaska's many special events. For dates and information, contact the Alaska Division of Tourism (address and phone in For More Information section).

FEBRUARY

Anchorage: Fur Rendezvous. **Cordova**: Iceworm Festival. **Delta Junction**: Festival of Lights. **Fairbanks**: Yukon Quest Sled Dog Race. **Nenana**: Tripod Raising Festival. **Sodotna**: Peninsula Winter Games, 10-Dog Classic Sled Dog Race.

MARCH

Anchorage: Iditarod Trail Sled Dog Race. **Fairbanks**: Winter Carnival, North American Sled Dog Championships. **Nome**: Iditarod Month, Bering Sea Ice Classic Golf Tournament. **North Pole**: Winter Carnival.

APRIL

Girdwood: Alyeska Spring Carnival. **Juneau**: Alaska Folk Festival. **Shishmaref**: Spring Carnival.

MAY

Barrow: Nalukataq Festival. **Cordova**: Copper River Delta Shorebird Festival. **Delta Junction**: Buffalo Wallow Square Dance Jamboree. **Glennallen**: Gulkana Air Show. **Homer**: Kachemak Bay Shorebird Festival. **Kodiak**: Crab Festival. **Nome**: Polar Bear Swim. **Petersburg**: Little Norway Festival. **Talkeetna**: Miners' Day Festival. **Tok**: Tanana 100 Boat Race.

JUNE

Anchorage: Mayor's Midnight Sun Marathon. **Fairbanks**: Midnight Sun Baseball Game, Yukon 800 Marathon Boat Race. **Haines**: Summer Solstice Celebration, Chilkat Bike Relay Race. **Juneau**: Gold Rush Days. **Nenana**: River Daze. **Nome**: Midnight Sun Festival. **Palmer**: Colony Days. **Sitka**: All-Alaska Logging Championships, Summer Music Festival.

JULY

Big Lake: Regatta. **Chugiak-Eagle River**: Bear Paw Festival. **Delta Junction**: Buffalo Barbecue, Deltana Fair. **Fairbanks**: Summer Arts Festival, Golden Days, World Eskimo-Indian Olympics. **Kotzebue**: Northwest Native Trade Fair. **Seward**: Mount Marathon Race. **Soldotna**: Progress Days. **Talkeetna**: Moose Dropping Festival.

AUGUST

Delta Junction: Deltana Fair. **Fairbanks**: Tanana Valley State Fair. **Haines**: Southeast Alaska State Fair. **Ketchikan**: Blueberry Arts Festival. **Kodiak**: Kodiak State Fair and Rodeo. **Ninilchik**: Kenai Peninsula State Fair. **Palmer**: Alaska State Fair. **Seward**: Silver Salmon Derby.

SEPTEMBER

Fairbanks: Equinox Marathon, Tanana Rampart Boat Race. **Haines**: Bald

Eagle Music Festival. **Homer**: Seafood Festival. **Kodiak**: State Fair and Rodeo. **Nome**: Golf Tournament, Great Bathtub Race. **Skagway**: Trail of '98 Road Relay to Whitehorse, YT. **Tok**: Tanana 100 Boat Races.

OCTOBER

Kenai: Annual Wine Tasting Festival. **Kodiak**: Oktoberfest. **Petersburg**: Seafood Festival, Oktoberfest. **Sitka**: Alaska Day Festival.

NOVEMBER

Anchorage: Great Alaska Shootout. **Fairbanks**: Top of the World Basketball Classic, Northern Invitational Curling Speil. **Haines**: Alaska Bald Eagle Festival.

◆ Exxon Valdez

The largest tanker spill in United States history occurred shortly after midnight on March 24, 1989, when the T/V *Exxon Valdez* ran aground on Bligh Reef in Prince William Sound. The ship spilled more than eleven million gallons of North Slope crude oil, which covered and contaminated portions of the shoreline of Prince William Sound, the Kenai Peninsula, lower Cook Inlet, the Kodiak Archipelago and the Alaska Peninsula, almost 600 miles southwest from the spill site. Affected areas included a national forest, four national wildlife refuges, three national parks, five state parks, four state critical-habitat areas and a state game sanctuary.

The immediate response to the spill focused on containment and clean up. Skimmers helped remove oil from the water; booms were positioned to keep oil from salmon hatcheries in Prince William Sound and Kodiak. Several thousand workers cleaned shorelines by hand or with high-pressure hot-water washing. In a process known as bioremediation, fertilizers were applied to some contaminated shorelines to increase the activity of oil-metabolizing microbes.

Estimates of wildlife killed by the spill vary. Several hundred thousand murres, bald eagles, loons, cormorants, grebes and other birds were killed. Studies estimate 3,500 to 5,500 sea otters and 200 harbor seals died. Status reports conducted six years after the spill show that the oil continues to cause contamination problems, especially in mussel beds. Although bald eagles seem to have fully recovered, other species such as the Pacific herring and harbor seal are in significant decline.

Exxon Corp. spent an estimated $2.5 billion on the cleanup, in addition to settling federal and state lawsuits and thousands of private claims.

◆ Fairbanks

In 1901, Capt. E.T. Barnette traveled up the Yukon River by steamer, planning to establish a trading post at Tanana Crossing (present-day Tanacross), the halfway point on the Valdez-to-Eagle Trail. But the quick current and shallow depths of the Tanana River prevented the steamer from navigating beyond the mouth of the Chena River. The ship's captain finally dropped off the irritated and protesting Barnette on the banks of the Chena, where he set up a temporary post.

One year later, an Italian prospector, Felix Pedro, discovered gold in nearby hills. The opportunistic Barnette abandoned his idea of continuing on to Tanana Crossing and the stampede of miners that followed in 1903-4 resulted in the newly incorporated city of Fairbanks.

Barnette's friend, Judge James Wickersham, named the town for Sen. Charles Fairbanks of Indiana, who later became vice president under Theodore Roosevelt. In 1903, Wickersham moved the headquarters of his Third Judicial District Court (which oversaw a 300,000-square-mile area) to Fairbanks, making it an administrative center. Barnette remained in Fairbanks, wheeling and dealing and serving as mayor until 1911, when one of his ventures, the Washington-Alaska Bank, failed. Barnette's colorful personality and entrepreneurial spirit earned him the nickname, "the most hated man in Fairbanks."

Present-day Fairbanks (pop. 30,843) is Alaska's second-largest city and the administrative capital of the Interior. The city is a service and supply point for industrial activities in the Interior and Arctic. In 1915, the city received an economic boost with the building of the Alaska Railroad, and later with the building of Fort Wainwright and Eielson Air Force Base. Fairbanks also experienced a huge, but temporary, boom during construction of the trans-Alaska pipeline in the 1970s. It is home to the University of Alaska at Fairbanks, which hosts an agricultural experiment station, a geophysical institute and an Alaska Native language program. The annual World Eskimo-Indian Olympics are held at Fairbanks, and Alaskaland Pioneer Park, constructed for Alaska's centennial celebration, is located nearby.

See also *Alaska Railroad, Alaskaland Pioneer Park, Fairbanks Exploration Co., Military Bases, Trans-Alaska Pipeline, Judge James Wickersham & World Eskimo-Indian Olympics.*

◆ Fairbanks Exploration Co. (F.E. Co.)

Between 1926 and 1957, the Fairbanks Exploration Co. removed an estimated $70 million in gold from the Fairbanks area. The F.E. Co. opened three dredges in 1929, and eventually operated eight dredges and numerous small hydraulic plants.

The company flourished until 1941, when the United States entered World War II. Production fell more than $2 million that year. The mining boom ceased almost immediately as gold mining was determined to be "nonstrategic" by wartime planners. After the war, rapidly rising costs forced many mines to remain closed.

Relics of the prosperous F.E. Co. include the Chena Pump House National Historic Site, built between 1931 and 1933 to pump water from the Chena River for dredging operations at Cripple Creek, and Davidson Ditch, an 83-mile-long system of ditches and inverted siphons built in 1925 to carry water to gold dredges. The line was capable of carrying 56,100 gallons per minute; after the F.E. Co. shut down, the water was used for power until a flood in 1967 destroyed almost 1,000 feet of pipe.

See also *Fairbanks, Gold & Mining.*

◆ Ferries

See *Alaska Marine Highway.*

◆ Fireweed

Fireweed thrives in Alaska's rugged terrain, growing in gravel riverbanks and in land cleared by people or ravaged by fire. Its magenta blossoms begin to show in early spring, and buds along the stalk continue to bloom until late summer, dropping off the stalk from the bottom to the top as winter approaches. Fireweed (*Epilobium angustifolium*) grows to 9 feet. The low-growing dwarf fireweed (*Epilobium latifolium*) frequently occurs on river bars and is commonly called river beauty.

◆ Fish Wheel

Introduced to Alaska in the early 1900s, and used by both Natives and early settlers, fish wheels are a fixed, rotating device for catching fish that is driven by river current or other means of power. Fish wheels are widely used for subsistence salmon fishing and some commercial salmon fishing.

Frank Whaley Photo

◆ Fishing

Commercial fishing is one of Alaska's oldest industries, dating back to the establishment of the first salmon cannery at Klawock in 1878. Alaska accounts for most of the salmon landed commercially in the U.S., and salmon is the leading fish in terms of value in the state's commercial fishing industry. Groundfish, in particular pollock, is second in value but first in volume, with 3 to 4 billion pounds of pollock caught annually compared to 8 to 9 million pounds of salmon.

The principal commercial fishing regions are Southeast, Prince William Sound, Cook Inlet, Gulf of Alaska, Kodiak, Aleutians, Bristol Bay and Bering Sea. Kodiak and Dutch Harbor are the chief fishing ports; Ketchikan and Petersburg are also important ports.

Other important commodities in Alaska's seafood industry, aside from salmon and groundfish (pollock and cod), are shellfish (King, snow and Dungeness crab, shrimp, scallops, clams), halibut and herring.

Alaska is also famous for its excellent sportfishing opportunities. About 70 percent of sportfishing occurs in the southcentral region, where most of the population lives. About half of Alaska's recreational anglers are visitors from outside the state. The most popular fish is salmon; but anglers also come for the trout (rainbow, steelhead and cutthroat), char (arctic, brook, lake and Dolly Varden), burbot, grayling, halibut and pike, among others. Catch-and-release fishing is popular, as anglers are able to land so many fish, and ice fishing is also practiced by many residents and visitors. For information on fishing and fish licenses, the Alaska Department of Fish and Game is a good resource (address and phone in For More Information section). Also, consult *The ALASKA WILDERNESS GUIDE*, available from Vernon Publications.

See also *Bristol Bay, Canneries, Industry, Ketchikan, Naknek, Ninilchik, Petersburg, Salmon & Unalaska (Dutch Harbor).*

✦ Flag

See *State Symbols.*

✦ Fords Terror

See *Tracy Arm-Fords Terror Wilderness Area*

✦ Fort Yukon

Fort Yukon (pop. 580), a bush village at the confluence of the Porcupine and Yukon rivers, is a hub for the Yukon Flats area. The community began in 1847, when a Hudson's Bay Co. trading post was founded near its present site. After the U.S. purchase of Alaska in 1867, Fort Yukon, near the Canada border, was determined to be within U.S. territory. By 1873, Francois Mercier, a trader with the Alaska Commercial Co., had established a post there.

The Klondike gold rush significantly increased river traffic, and Fort Yukon's population grew. As white people moved to the area, local Athabascan people suffered greatly from diseases they brought with them. For years, Fort Yukon was the largest settlement on the Yukon downriver from Dawson. The pioneer missionary Hudson Stuck is buried in Fort Yukon.

See also *Alaska Commercial Co., Athabascans, Gold & Hudson Stuck.*

✦ Fossils

Alaska's cold climate and the deep-freeze characteristics of permafrost terrain offer near-perfect conditions for the preservation of fossils. Many prehistoric beasts' remains, such as the wooly mammoth, have been discovered, excellently preserved, in permafrost.

One of the premier names in Alaskan paleontology, Dr. Otto Geist, donated most of his fossil collection to the University of Alaska Museum.

He gathered fossils on St. Lawrence Island and in the Fairbanks area. As gold dredging operations turned over land in creeks in and around Fairbanks, Geist worked out an agreement with a mining company, the university and the American Museum of Natural History. He arranged for miners to send for him immediately if pieces of ancient bone surfaced during their work. He would hurry to the site and excavate immediately; then mining would continue.

See also *Dinosaurs*.

◆ Fox Farming

The fox farming industry began with the Russian-American Co.'s introduction of foxes to the Aleutian Islands, which had no indigenous population. In 1879 (after the U.S. purchase of Alaska), the Secretary of the Treasury began an island leasing program for fox farmers, and the industry gained popularity. Both red and arctic foxes were farmed.

The arctic fox, valued for its blue-color phase, could survive with little help on many islands. The fox scavenged for food and was fairly easy for the farmer to capture at pelting time. The red fox, however, was more elusive and difficult to capture, so farmers tended to raise red foxes in pens. Usually, pen-raised fox had higher quality pelts.

Farming of other furbearing animals, such as the lynx and wolverine, was attempted, but fox farming proved the most profitable. The industry peaked in 1929, and collapsed with the Great Depression. Many of the fox farming islands were damaged by the influx of non-native foxes. For instance, the Aleutian Canada goose, whose eggs were a dietary staple for many foxes, is now an endangered species. The federal government has invested money to try to undo some of the damage.

See also *Aleutian Islands, Foxes, Fur Trapping & Russian-American Co.*

◆ Foxes

Two types of fox live in Alaska: the arctic fox and the red fox. The red fox commonly has a reddish-golden coat, though some animals are black, silver or a combination. The red fox is found throughout the state, except in Southeast and around Prince William Sound in Southcentral. The arctic fox has a variety of possible color combinations. Two general phases—blue or white—exist; the white-phase fox is brownish-gray on top and white or sandy underneath in summer, while in winter its coat turns completely white. The blue-phase fox ranges from bluish-gray in winter to brown in summertime. Found along the Arctic coast and more recently in the Pribilof and Aleutian islands, the arctic fox is similar in size (6-15 pounds) to the red.

See also *Fox Farming.*

◆ Frost Heaves and Boils

A frost heave is a bump or crack in a paved road; this ruptured pavement occurs when water in the ground beneath freezes and expands. Another detrimental condition—frost boils—occurs in gravel or dirt roads when the ground begins to thaw, leaving soft spots in the road.

◆ Fur Rendezvous

See *Anchorage Fur Rendezvous.*

◆ Fur Trapping

Alaska has 19 species of furbearers, including minks, wolves, foxes, wolverines, lynx, marten and beavers. Beaver and mink furs have traditionally brought the highest prices because of their durability and light weight.

In the early years of Russian occupation, hunters focused their efforts on the sea otter and fur seal, whose pelts were extremely valuable. As British and American trading companies became active, it was primarily Natives who trapped animals for the white traders. But the late-19th-century gold rushes brought an increase of white miners and prospectors, many of whom trapped during the winter months to supplement their incomes.

Throughout the years, a number of modern innovations have changed trapping methods. Trappers use steel traps and snares instead of wooden ones, and many travel their lines by snowmobile instead of by dog sled or on foot. Most of Alaska's furs are harvested in the Yukon and Kuskokwim valleys, although trapping takes place throughout the state.

This historic trade continues to be a viable means of making a living for some people in the Bush. Trapping is regulated by the State Department of Fish and Game.

See also *Beavers, Fox Farming, Muskrats, Promyshlenniki, Russian-American Co. & Subsistence.*

◆ Gates of the Arctic National Park and Preserve

Established in 1980, 8.4-million-acre Gates of the Arctic National Park and Preserve lies north of the Arctic Circle, covering the crest of the Brooks Range. In 1924, forester Robert Marshall, who was exploring the unmapped area, noted "a precipitous pair of mountains, one on each side of the North Fork (Koyukuk River)," and he "bestowed the name of 'Gates of the Arctic' on them, christening the east portal 'Boreal Mountain' and the west portal 'Frigid Crags.'"

Within the park and preserve, Athabascan and Eskimo peoples continue to pursue a traditional subsistence lifestyle. The area is rich in wildlife, hosting 36 mammal species from the hoary marmot to the moose, and a variety of migratory birds and eagles. Activities include floating the six wild and scenic rivers that flow through the park (Alatna, John, Kobuk, Noatak, North Fork of the Koyukuk and Tinayguk), rock and mountain climbing and hiking.

See also *National Parklands.*

✦ Ghost Towns

The remains of many abandoned boom towns may be found through-out Alaska. Former Russian villages (such as Belkofski), trading posts (such as Chandalar and Kemperville) and mining camps (including Diamond, Mastodon and Nation) offer glimpses into Alaska's rich frontier history. Access to the towns is usually limited at best, and many are on private property. Some, such as Glacier, a 1920s mining town in Denali National Park and Preserve with a number of old homes and warehouses, are easiest to visit during the winter when overland access is possible; Glacier is virtually in-visible from the air when leaves are on the trees. For further information, consult *The ALASKA WILDERNESS GUIDE* (available from Vernon Publica-tions). Also, contact the Alaska Division of Tourism (address and phone number in For More Information section).

✦ Giardiasis

Giardia is a microscopic organism found in some of Alaska's seemingly pristine river, lake and stream waters. It causes severe intestinal discomfort when ingested by humans. Giardiasis may be avoided by boiling all drink-ing and cooking water used in the wilderness.

✦ Glacier Bay National Park and Preserve

Some of the world's most impressive tidewater glaciers are found in Glacier Bay, making it one of the top five visitor attractions in Alaska. The area is experiencing the most rapid retreat of glaciers since the Ice Age. Near the northern end of the Alaska Panhandle, Glacier Bay is bordered by Icy Strait and Cross Sound on the south, the Gulf of Alaska on the west and Canada on the north. First recognized as a national monument in 1925, Glacier Bay was later made a national park and preserve in 1980.

Mt. Fairweather, in the towering Fairweather Range, is 15,300 feet, and was sighted and named by Capt. James Cook in 1778. Attractions in the park include the unspoiled coastline and wildlife, such as whales, seals, brown and black bears, mountain goats, moose and eagles. More than 225 bird species have been sighted.

The naturalist John Muir first canoed through Glacier Bay in 1879. He built a cabin at what is now Muir Point. Muir Glacier, just to the north of the point, has receded 25 miles in the years since Muir was there.

Popular activities today include canoeing, and boating; hiking, backpack-ing and mountaineering; and sightseeing by way of cruises and guided hikes.

See also *Glaciers & National Parklands.*

♦ Glaciers

Alaska has more than 5,000 glaciers, including the two largest glaciers in North America—Bering and Malaspina. Both these glaciers are larger in area than the state of Delaware, approximately 2,900 square miles each. Of the top 10 most-visited attractions in Alaska, No. 1 is Portage Glacier (almost half of all visitors see it); No. 3 is Mendenhall Glacier; and No. 4, Glacier Bay.

Glaciers are formed in high mountains when the amount of winter snowfall exceeds the summer melt. As the snow accumulates, its weight causes ice crystals to fuse, forming glacial ice. The ice flows at a rate determined by gravity, temperature, precipitation and other geologic forces. Some glaciers remain stationary for long periods of time, while others advance or retreat relatively quickly. When a glacier advances, it destroys all plant life in its path; after the ice melts, vegetation grows in the sediment left behind.

Tidewater glaciers *calve*—form icebergs by delivering masses of broken-off ice into water at their *terminus* (ending point). When retreating, glaciers also leave behind *moraine*—drift or sediment, and carve *fjords*— deep, U-shaped valleys. Some glaciers have *nunataks*—mountain peaks that poke through the ice.

See also *Glacier Bay National Park, Ice Fields, Icebergs and Valdez; & Bering, Columbia, Hubbard, Malaspina, Matanuska, Mendenhall and Portage glaciers.*

♦ Glennallen

Glennallen (pop. 451) lies at the western edge of the massive Wrangell-St. Elias National Park and Preserve. Glennallen is a gateway to the Wrangell Mountains and service center for the Copper River region. Its name was derived from the combined last names of Capt. Edwin Forbes Glenn and Lt. Henry Tureman Allen, both leaders in exploration of the Copper River region in the late 1800s.

See also *Wrangell-St. Elias National Park and Preserve.*

♦ Gold

Gold, found in three main areas of Alaska—the central Yukon River basin, Southeast and southern Seward Peninsula—has been luring opportunists to Alaska for more than 100 years. Great expanses of wilderness, known previously only by Natives, were opened by gold strikes near the turn of the century in Juneau (1880), Circle City (1893), Klondike (Yukon Territory, 1896), Nome (1898) and Fairbanks (1902). The strikes were followed by stampedes of gold-seekers, drawn by the stories of great riches. Alaska's modern economic development began with these large influxes of prospectors. Other significant strikes include: Fortymile (1866), Innoko (1906), Ruby (1907), Iditarod (1909), Marshall and Chisana (1913) and Livengood (1914).

Three of the largest gold nuggets ever discovered in Alaska were all found within one month's time near Nome. On Sept. 5, 1901, a 45-ounce nugget was found on the Jarvis Brothers' claim on Anvil Creek. On Sept. 14, on Discovery Claim, a 97-ounce nugget was uncovered. Then on Sept. 29, the largest gold nugget on record in Alaska was found at this same claim. It was 7 inches long by 4 inches wide and weighed 107 ounces.

In 1968, the Alaska Legislature adopted gold as the Alaska state mineral.

See also *Anvil Creek, Council, Chilkoot Pass, Fairbanks, Ghost Towns, Juneau, The Kink, Klondike Gold Rush Historical Park, Minerals, Nome, Skagway & Russian John Zarnowsky.*

◆ Good Friday Earthquake

Alaska's most famous earthquake, the Good Friday Earthquake, occurred at 5:36 p.m. on March 27, 1964, and lasted an unusually long four minutes. Centered in the Prince William Sound area, it wiped out the small town of Chenega on the south tip of Chenega Island in Prince William Sound. (After years of effort by former Chenega residents, the new town of Chenega Bay was dedicated in 1984.) The community of Portage at the end of Turnagain Arm in Cook Inlet was also destroyed when the ground sank 10 feet. The earthquake destroyed docks and warehouses in the ports of Seward, Valdez, Kodiak and Whittier, while Anchorage suffered millions of dollars in damage.

People felt shock waves 700 miles away, and tidal waves as far away as Oregon and California killed 14 people. Alaska's death toll was 131 people. If the quake had occurred during school and business hours, that number would have been far higher.

See also *Earthquakes.*

◆ Great Kobuk Sand Dunes

See *Kobuk Valley National Park.*

◆ Ernest Gruening

Ernest Gruening, territorial governor of Alaska from 1939-53, was a strong proponent of statehood. As Alaskans began a campaign to become the 49th state in the union, two ghost senators were chosen by the Alaska constitutional convention to represent their efforts in U.S. Congress; one was William A. Egan, the other, Ernest Gruening.

See also *William A. Egan & Statehood.*

◆ Gulf of Alaska

The Gulf of Alaska, an inlet of the Pacific Ocean, lies between the Alaska Peninsula and the Alexander Archipelago in southeastern Alaska. The 592,000-square-mile gulf is known for its violent storms; its major ports are Anchorage, Seward and Valdez.

✦ Haida Indians

The Haida Indians are believed to have created the art of totem pole carving. Thought to have migrated from the British Columbia area to Southeast 400 to 500 years ago, today they occupy the Queen Charlotte Islands in British Columbia and Prince of Wales Island, Alaska.

The Haida Indians share some cultural similarities with the Tlingit and Tsimshian peoples. All rely on the forest and the sea for their subsistence and spirituality; and unlike other Alaska Natives, they had capitalist, not socialist, societies.

In 1911, the town of Hydaburg was founded on the southwest coast of Prince of Wales Island. It combined the populations of three Haida villages: Sukkwan, Howkan and Klinkwan. President William Howard Taft designated the surrounding land an Indian reservation in 1912, but in 1926, residents of Hydaburg asked that it be restored to its former status as part of the Tongass National Forest.

Today, Hydaburg (pop. 384) has a fishing-based economy, and subsistence methods continue to be a necessary part of life. Hydaburg has an excellent collection of restored Haida totem poles on display in a totem park developed by the Civilian Conservation Corps in the 1930s.

See also *Carving and Sculpture, Natives, Tlingit Indians, Tsimshians & Totem Poles.*

◆ Haines

The Chilkat Valley was first inhabited by Tlingit Indians, who vigorously defended their inland trading routes from new arrivals. In 1881, the Presbyterian missionary S. Hall Young established a mission at the present site of Haines on the Alaska Panhandle. The mission evolved into a township as gold mining began in the Porcupine District, upriver from Haines, and the town became a supply point and outlet.

The Klondike gold rush of 1898 brought a further influx of gold-seekers, who opened up the Chilkat Mountain Pass to the Interior. In 1904, the U.S. government established Fort William H. Seward in Haines, which was renamed Chilkoot Barracks in 1922 and deactivated in 1946. As a mainline port on the Alaska Marine Highway and one of only three Southeast communities on the Alaska Highway (the others are Hyder and Skagway), Haines (pop. 1,238) remains an important route to the Interior.

See also *Chilkoot Trail & Gold.*

◆ Halibut

See *Deep Creek, Fishing & Homer.*

◆ Hares

Two species of hares live in Alaska—the northern, or tundra, hare and the abundant snowshoe hare. The northern hare is found along the north and west coasts of Alaska. In winter the northern hare is completely white, with the exception of the tips of its ears, which are black. In summer the hare is brownish-gray. With willow as its main foodstuff, the northern hare may weigh more than 12 pounds, and be 2-1/2 feet tall. They prefer to live on tundra and rocky slopes.

The snowshoe hare is much smaller—weighing just three to four pounds. Snowshoes are found in many areas of the state. Similar in coloring to the northern hare, the snowshoe is pure white in winter; in summer it is a combination of grayish-brown and white, with black and reddish markings. Its population fluctuates greatly, in cycles of roughly 10 years. Lynx are the snowshoe hares' main predator—though animals as diverse as hawks and wolverines feed on them, and for humans, they are a popular small game species. Snowshoe hares earned their name from their well-adapted feet, which are covered in coarse hair that works like a snowshoe, allowing them to cross deep, light snow.

✦ Harriman Alaska Expedition

In 1899, the railroad magnate Edward H. Harriman (1848-1909) organized what was to be the last great expedition of the 19th century and the end of the era of discovery in Alaska. Accompanying Harriman aboard the *George W. Elder* were William Healy Dall, who had surveyed much of Alaska's coast with the U.S. Coast and Geodetic Survey during the 1870s and '80s; naturalist John Muir; photographer Edward S. Curtis; and a mining engineer named W.B. Devereux. The voyage provided a wealth of scientific information in 13 volumes of reports detailing their findings. The expedition named Columbia Glacier, but discovered only one new landmark, a fjord northeast of Whittier, which they named Harriman Fjord.

✦ Walter J. Hickel

Walter J. Hickel served as the state's second governor (Republican) from 1966 to January 1969, when he resigned to become Secretary of the Interior. He was re-elected governor of Alaska in 1990, the seventh governor since Alaska became a state in 1959, and the first governor of the Alaska Independent Party.

✦ William Hensley

William "Willie" Hensley, an Inupiat Eskimo, was instrumental in the creation of the Alaska Federation of Natives and the resulting land-claims action against the federal government. Hensley headed the NANA Regional Corp. and helped develop Red Dog zinc mine. He is commissioner of the Alaska Depart. of Commerce and Economic Development.

✦ Highways

Alaska's highway system links communities in Southcentral and the Interior with the Alaska Highway from Canada. Southeast Alaska also has an extensive system of roads, but most do not connect with one another and only the Haines Highway and Klondike Highway 2 connect with the mainland highway system in Canada.

The main highway system includes 200 miles of the Alaska Highway between the Canadian border and Delta Junction; the 323-mile George Parks Highway, Anchorage to Fairbanks; the 162-mile Steese Highway, Fairbanks to Circle; the 152-mile Elliott Highway, Fox to Manley Hot Springs; the 160-mile Taylor Highway to Eagle; the 328-mile Glenn

Highway/Tok Cutoff, Tok to Anchorage; the 136-mile Denali Highway, Paxson to Cantwell; the 368-mile Richardson Highway, Valdez to Fairbanks; the 35-mile Edgerton Highway to Chitina; the 127-mile Seward Highway, Anchorage to Seward; and the 143-mile Sterling Highway to Homer. The 414-mile Dalton Highway connects Fairbanks with Prudhoe Bay on the Arctic coast. Not connected to this system is the 48-mile Copper River Highway (Route 10) from Cordova, which deadends at the Million Dollar Bridge.

Most major highways are paved, with the exception of the Dalton, Elliott and Taylor highways, and portions of the Denali, Copper River and Steese highways, which are gravel. For mile-by-mile logs of all northern highways, consult *The MILEPOST®* (Vernon Publications Inc.).

See also *Alaska Highway, Copper River Highway & Dalton Highway.*

◆ Hiking

Alaska State Parks, the U.S. Forest Service and the Bureau of Land Management maintain most of the established trails within Alaska. Within the state park system, Chugach State Park near Anchorage has the most extensive trail system, with more than 200 miles of hiking trails. Chugach National Forest offers some 200 miles of trail, including the 70-mile-long Resurrection Trail system on the Kenai Peninsula. Tongass National Forest has almost 600 miles of trails. Most national parklands have no established trail systems, instead offering cross-country hiking or—depending on the terrain—bushwacking. An exception is the 33-mile Chilkoot Trail out of Skagway managed by the National Park Service. The BLM's White Mountains National Recreation Area north of Fairbanks has more than 200 miles of winter trails and 20 miles of summer hiking trails. The BLM also manages the 27-mile Pinnell Mountain National Recreation Trail in Steese National Conservation Area outside Fairbanks. Only small portions of the 1,000-mile Iditarod National Historic Trail, surveyed in 1910 as the Seward to Nome Mail Trail, are suitable for summer hiking.

◆ Homer

Homer (pop. 3,660), the "Halibut Fishing Capital of the World," is on the southwestern edge of the Kenai Peninsula on Kachemak Bay near the mouth of the Cook Inlet. Homer's mild climate, picturesque setting and great fishing attract thousands of visitors each year. Commercial fishing is a key part of its economy.

From June to September the bluffs behind Homer are colored with the blooms of fireweed, lupine and paintbrush. The Homer Spit, a long, gravel bar, stretches 5 miles out from the shore. During the 1964 earthquake, the Spit sank more than 4 feet, requiring several buildings to be moved to higher ground.

See also *Good Friday Earthquake.*

◆ Homesteading

Alaska's federal homesteading laws were repealed in 1986. Although the federal government offers no "free" land, the state does dispose of some acreage free-of-cost to residents who are willing to survey, occupy and improve the land. Also, nonagricultural land is sometimes available (and sold at market value) to buyers who agree to stake, survey and clear brush off it. Alaska's 365 million acres are owned by the federal government, the state, Native claims and private individuals.

◆ Hooligan

Hooligan, a smelt that grows up to nine inches in length, are so oily that they are reputed to be a good source of lamp oil; hence, they are also known as Candlefish (and Eulachon). Hooligan are abundant in the Alaska Peninsula area.

◆ Molly Hootch

In 1976, a student named Molly Hootch won a court decision that said she and all other Alaskan children were entitled to the right to continue their education in their own villages. Up until this time, many Alaskan children from rural villages who wanted to go to high school had to leave home to do so. After Molly Hootch won the case, all communities with one or more persons of high school age were required to offer high school studies.

See also *Education.*

◆ Hot Springs

Alaska has many natural hot springs. The U.S. Geological Survey identifies 79 thermal springs in Alaska, about half of which are found along the volcanic Alaska Peninsula and Aleutian chain. Many communities near springs were populated around the turn of the century when miners were exploring Alaska's creeks in search of gold.

Some of the more well-known, and developed, springs are Chena, Tenakee Springs and Manley. Other springs include Circle and Melozi in the Interior; Baranof, Chief Shakes, Goddard, Shelokum, Trocadero and White Sulphur in Southeast; and Pilgrim and Serpentine in Western Alaska. For further information contact the Alaska Division of Tourism (address and phone in For More Information section), or consult *The ALASKA WILDERNESS GUIDE* (available from Vernon Publications).

◆ Hubbard Glacier

In June 1986, Hubbard Glacier made news when it advanced so rapidly that it sealed off Russell Fjord, creating a freshwater lake out of the saltwater inlet. This sudden ecological change in "Russell Lake" threatened fish and plant species and trapped seals and porpoises. Attempts to rescue the mammals failed, but by October the glacier dam broke, allowing the fjord to heal itself.

The 80-mile-long glacier, which has its terminus in Yakutat Bay in Southeast, has made 10 significant advances and retreats since the Ice Age ended about 10,000 years ago.

See also *Glaciers.*

◆ Hunting

Sportsmen come from all over the world to hunt Alaska's big game species: brown (grizzly) and black bears, caribou, Dall sheep, moose, mountain goats, Sitka black-tailed deer, wolves, bison, elk, musk oxen and wolverines. Waterfowl are also abundant, including geese, cranes, ducks and snipe. At present, no hunting of polar bears or marine mammals is allowed.

Hunters must abide by the many rules and regulations of the state and federal governments, including those governing permits, licenses, tickets, stamps, tags, seals and reports. For further information on rules and regulations, contact the Alaska Department of Fish and Game. For information on hunting guides, contact the Alaska Division of Tourism or refer to advertisements Alaskan guides have placed in *The MILEPOST®* (available from Vernon Publications). (Addresses and phone numbers are available in For More Information section).

See also *Bears, Bison, Caribou, Dall Sheep, Deer, Elk, Moose, Mountain Goats, Musk Oxen, Wolves & Wolverines.*

"It is in the Alaskan Range that nature assumes the heroic, that the last battle of the mountains appears to have been fought. These great towering volcanic peaks and the quaking islands are superb beyond description, filling the breast of the beholder with awe. And the ground about, though cold enough upon the surface, steams and sweats in sympathy, manifesting its internal warmth in geysers and hot springs, while from the depths of the sea sometimes belches forth fire, if certain navigators may be believed, and the sky blazes in northern lights."

— *H.H. Bancroft*

◆ Ice Fields

More than 28,000 square miles of Alaska are covered by ice fields—about 4 percent of the state. Most are found in the Alaska Range and Wrangell Mountains, and in the mountains of Southeast. Some of Alaska's larger ice fields are the Juneau, Stikine and Harding ice fields; each is between 500 and 1,500 square miles, and is drained by numerous tributary glaciers.

See also *Glaciers, Juneau Icefield & Kenai Fjords National Park (Harding Icefield).*

◆ Ice Fog

Ice fog—a thick white fog, made of ice crystals—occurs when extremely cold air (-22°F or below) mixes with moist vapors. Ice fogs are common in the wintertime in Fairbanks, which is surrounded by hills that prevent winds from clearing the air. The fog may last for more than a week and is often compounded by car exhaust and industrial pollution in the city.

See also *Fairbanks.*

◆ Icebergs

Alaska's icebergs are relatively small in comparison with those found near Greenland and Antarctica. Icebergs are most commonly seen in areas of southcentral and southeastern Alaska, such as Prince William Sound,

Glacier and Yakutat bays, Endicott Arm and Mendenhall and Portage lakes. They are formed when ice breaks off the terminus of a glacier into a body of water—a process known as calving. Icebergs (even when found in salt water) are made of fresh water; they occur wherever glaciers extend into the sea or a freshwater lake.

See also *Glaciers & Sea Ice.*

◆ Iceworms

Iceworms, which were long regarded as fictitious, are small black worms that live in temperatures just above freezing. The only members of the earthworm family known to live in snow or ice, iceworms generally grow to no more than 1 inch in length. They eat algae, and are food for several species of birds. Iceworms were first reported on Muir Glacier in 1887.

See also *Portage Glacier.*

◆ Iditarod Trail Sled Dog Race

The Iditarod Trail Sled Dog Race is a major annual sporting event in Alaska. The first race—a 56-mile-course run in 1967—was conceived and organized by musher Joe Redington Sr. of Knik and historian Dorothy Page of Wasilla. In 1973, the trail was lengthened to 1,100 miles, with the race starting in Anchorage on March 3 and ending on April 3 in Nome. Of the 34 mushers who started the 1973 race, 22 finished.

In 1976, Congress designated the Iditarod as a National Historic Trail. Following the dog team mail route blazed in 1910 from Knik to Nome, the trail crosses two mountain ranges, runs along the Yukon River for about 150 miles, goes through several bush villages and crosses the pack ice of Norton Sound. The trail is passable only in winter; in summer much of the ground thaws to spongy muskeg swamp.

The route attracted national attention in 1925, when sled dog mushers, including the famous Leonhard Seppala, relayed 300,000 units of life-saving diphtheria serum to epidemic-threatened Nome. In later years, the snowmobile and airplane replaced dog teams as means of transport, and the trail fell into disuse. Through Redington's efforts, the Iditarod Trail has been assured a place in Alaska history.

Each year mushers race their teams from the starting line in Anchorage to Eagle River, where they load the teams onto trucks to Settler's Bay in Wasilla, where the race officially begins. They head out into the Bush, and more than 1,000 miles later arrive at the finish line in Nome. On odd-numbered years the race takes an alternate route south. While the route traditionally is described as 1,049 miles long (a figure selected because Alaska is the 49th state), its actual length is close to 1,100 miles. The Iditarod has been run every year since its inception. For further information contact the Iditarod Trail Committee (address in For More Information section).

See also *Dog Mushing, Libby Riddles & Sled Dogs.*

◆ Igloos

Igloos are often associated with Alaska Eskimos, but in fact, igloos are a type of housing used by Canadian Eskimos. Eskimo hunters in Alaska occasionally use temporary snow shelters for emergency housing during storms.

◆ Iliamna Lake

Iliamna Lake, along with nearby Lake Clark and tributary rivers, helps support the world's largest sockeye (red) salmon run. The salmon grow to maturity in Bristol Bay and swim up the Kvichak River to spawn. Located at the northern end of the Alaska Peninsula, Iliamna is the state's largest lake. It covers 1,000 square miles and is 75 miles long, 20 miles wide and 1,000 feet deep.

The lake has many other fish species in abundance (including king, silver and pink salmon, and Dolly Varden, char, trout and grayling), making it a popular fishing ground. The town of Iliamna (pop. 119), on the north side of the lake, is a major gateway to world-class fishing and hunting on the Kvichak River drainage.

Iliamna Lake is also reputedly home to a sea monster. Natives, fishermen and residents of the surrounding villages claim to have seen the monster on several occasions. Some people speculate that the sightings were actually of an oversize sturgeon, a beluga whale or a giant squid.

See also *Bristol Bay, Fishing, Lakes & Salmon.*

◆ Industry

Alaska's main industries are petroleum, minerals, fisheries, forestry and tourism. Petroleum (refined into oil and gas) contributes almost 50 percent of the gross state product, though the number is on the decline. In comparison, fishing, forestry and mining combined contribute only about

6 percent of the gross product. Alaska ranks first among the states in the export of fisheries, second in the export of forest products and third in minerals. Government is one of the biggest employers in the state. Agriculture, including farming in the Matanuska and Tanana valleys, plays a small role in the state's economy.

See also *Agriculture, Fishing, Fur Trapping, Mining, Oil, Timber & Tourism.*

◆ Insects

Much like wilderness areas in other parts of the United States, Alaska has its share of pesky insects. Mosquitoes are perhaps the most widespread and persistent of insects in Alaska, occurring in Alaska's many miles of swampy tundra and lakes from early spring into the fall. Other pests include the black fly, present from May until freeze-up; the snipe fly, found during the summer months in mountainous regions as far north as the Alaska Range; and no-see-ums, swarms of which are found in coastal areas from June to August. Black flies, unlike most flying insects, are known to crawl underneath clothing; their bites may fester for as long as a week. The snipe fly's bite hurts more initially, but the effects don't last as long.

◆ Inside Passage

The Inside Passage refers to the protected waterways of Southeast, between the Alexander Archipelago and mainland. The Alaska Marine Highway System (the state's ferry system) operates between communities in Alaska's "panhandle," as do many private cruise ship companies. The area is forested with spruce and hemlock, and has hundreds of islands, fjords and inlets. The waters are home to a variety of sea mammals, including whales and porpoises. Cities and towns in the Inside Passage include Ketchikan, Wrangell, Petersburg, Juneau and Haines.

See also *Alaska Marine Highway, Alexander Archipelago, Haines, Juneau, Ketchikan, Panhandle, Petersburg & Wrangell.*

◆ Islands

Alaska has close to 2,000 named islands, rocks and reefs; of these, more than 1,000 are in Southeast. Kodiak (3,588 square miles) is the largest island in Alaska and the second largest island in the United States (after Hawaii). The next-largest islands are Prince of Wales (2,231 square miles),

Chichagof (2,062 square miles), St. Lawrence (1,780 square miles) and Admiralty (1,709 square miles).

See also *Afognak Island, Aleutian Islands, Alexander Archipelago, Diomede Islands, Kodiak Island, Nunivak Island, Pribilof Islands & St. Lawrence Island.*

◆ Ivory

The art of ivory carving by Alaska Eskimos continues a 2,000-year heritage. Most ivory carving is done by residents on the Seward Peninsula and the Bering Sea islands of Nunivak, St. Lawrence and Little Diomede, which have access to large herds of walrus that migrate through the Bering Sea. The ivory carvers use the tusks and teeth of walrus. Old walrus ivory is also recovered from ancient village sites and used for carving. According to the Marine Mammals Protection Act of 1972, only Natives can hunt walrus, and federal laws also govern the possession and sale of fresh walrus ivory, as well as old (fossil) and found (beach) walrus ivory, and mammoth and mastodon ivory. Fresh walrus ivory has a pink cast. Fossil ivory, which may have been buried in the ground or laying on the beach for years, is a pale creamy color with amber or yellow undertones and a streak of mottling. The rarest and most valued fossil ivory exhibits blue-black and sometimes gold tones, and comes from ancient sites exposed to saltwater. Imported elephant ivory has a distinctive cross-hatching or moire pattern.

The art of carving intricate designs on ivory is called scrimshaw. Early in the century, Nunivak islanders developed a unique form of scrimshaw in which entire walrus tusks are carved into intertwined animal figures, such as seals, whales, polar bears, foxes and walrus.

◆ Sheldon Jackson

Dr. Sheldon Jackson, a Presbyterian missionary, made numerous trips to Alaska throughout his lifetime to promote the educational and religious needs of Alaska Natives. In 1885, after writing a book and newsletters, and giving numerous lectures on the conditions of Alaska Natives, he was appointed U.S. general agent for education in Alaska, a position he held until 1906. Jackson approached other denominations for help in establishing schools. He also made an innovative effort to improve Native conditions, which had declined as white settlers and profiteers overhunted native animal species, by importing reindeer from Siberia. Natives could raise reindeer, a cousin of the caribou, for their meat and hides.

See also *Education & Reindeer.*

◆ Jade

See *State Symbols.*

◆ Juneau

Juneau (borough pop. 26,751), located on Gastineau Channel on mainland Southeast, was the site of the first gold rush on Alaska soil. In 1880, nearly 20 years before the great gold rushes to Klondike and Nome, two prospectors named Joseph Juneau and Richard Harris found pebble-sized gold nuggets in what is now called Gold Creek (a small, clear stream that runs through the center of present-day Juneau).

For two years, Juneau and Harris could not agree on what to name the town. Finally, a group of miners who were upset with Harris for staking multiple claims decided to name the town Juneau and the district Harrisburg. Juneau boomed as claims and mines sprang up throughout the area to exploit one of the largest lodes of gold quartz in the world.

For a time the largest mine was the Treadwell, across Gastineau Channel from Juneau, but in 1917 a cave-in and flood closed it. In 36 years of operation the Treadwell produced $66 million in gold. Another large mine, the Alaska-Gastineau Mine, had a 2-mile shaft through Mt. Roberts to the Perseverance Mine near Gold Creek. The largest and most prosperous of Juneau's mines was the Alaska-Juneau (A-J) Mine. Built into the heart of Mt. Roberts, it operated 58 years—producing $80 million in gold.

In 1900, given Juneau's growth and the simultaneous decline of Sitka (after the departure of the Russians and dwindling whaling and fur trades), it was decided to move the capital to Juneau. The transfer of government functions took place in 1906. Today, government comprises about half of Juneau's total industry.

Juneau, which is sometimes called "a little San Francisco," is the only state capital in the country that is not accessible by road. The presence of glaciers makes road-building impractical; air and water transport are used instead. Juneau is nestled at the foot and on the side of Mt. Juneau (3,576 feet). Mt. Roberts (3,819 feet) also rises above the city. A bridge across Gastineau Channel connects Juneau to Douglas—a town that was incorporated into the borough of Juneau in 1971.

Located in the Juneau area are the University of Alaska Southeast campus at Auke Bay, the State Capitol Building, the Alaska State Museum and the Governor's Mansion. Other sights include the House of Wickersham, the St. Nicholas Russian Orthodox Church (built in 1894, it is the oldest Russian Orthodox church in Southeast), Mendenhall Glacier (accessible by highway from downtown) and the Juneau Icefield.

See also *Alaska-Juneau Mine, Gold, Juneau Icefield, Mendenhall Glacier, Sitka, Judge James Wickersham & Willow.*

◆ Juneau Icefield

East of Juneau, along the crest of the Coast Range, the Juneau Icefield stretches from the Taku River to just east of Skagway. Covering about

1,200 square miles, the Juneau Icefield is the source of more than 30 valley glaciers, including Mendenhall, Taku, Eagle and Herbert. All of the glaciers, except for Taku, are retreating. The ice field is the most studied in Alaska, primarily through the Juneau Icefield Research Program (JIRP), established in the 1940s. The best way to view the ice field is by plane or helicopter.

See also *Glaciers & Ice Fields.*

♦ Kachemak Bay

In Aleut dialect, Kachemak is said to mean "smoky bay." The name supposedly derived from the smoke that once rose from smoldering coal seams jutting from clay bluffs on the north shore of Kachemak Bay and cliffs near Anchor Point. In early days, many of the exposed coal seams were slowly burning from unknown causes. Today, erosion of these bluffs causes huge fragments of coal to drop on the beaches, creating a plentiful supply of winter fuel for residents. An estimated 400 million tons of coal are deposited in the immediate vicinity of Homer.

Kachemak—a beautiful, 40-mile-long deep-water bay that reaches inland from Cook Inlet on the southwest coast of the Kenai Peninsula—is rich in marine life. The wild timbered coastline of the south shore, across from Homer, is indented with many fjords and inlets, reaching far into the Kenai Mountains. Kachemak Bay State Park is one of the largest and most scenic parks in the state system. The tides in Kachemak Bay are among the largest in the world, with an average vertical difference, between high and low tides, of 15 feet; extremes of 28 feet occur on large tide cycles.

See also *Homer.*

♦ Kake

Kake (pop. 700), on the northwest coast of Kupreanof Island in the Alexander Archipelago, has a 132-1/2-foot-tall totem, reputedly the tallest

"In the afternoon I sent Mr. King again with two armed boats, with orders to land on the northern point of the low land on the SE side of the River [Possession Point, Cook Inlet], there to display the flag [and] take possession of the Country and River in his Majesty's name..."

— Capt. James Cook

June 1778

in the world. It was carved for the 1967 Alaska Purchase Centennial Celebration.

Kake is a permanent village of the Kake tribe of the Tlingit Indians—a tribe renowned in the 18th and 19th centuries for its fierce and aggressive warriors. The Kakes earned this reputation primarily from two separate incidents.

In 1869, Kakes murdered two Sitka traders in revenge for the shooting of a Native by a sentry in Sitka. The United States responded by shelling three Kake villages, an event that came to be called the Kake War. It resulted in the destruction of 35 houses, two forts and many canoes, and the loss of winter food stores.

Earlier, in 1857, the Kake Indians had been involved in another skirmish, this time with the U.S. military in Washington state. After a party of Kakes made a 1,000-mile journey south to Puget Sound to pick hops, a U.S. military commander fired on them, killing a chief. The following year, the Kakes returned to seek retribution and slayed a U.S. Customs official, coming back to Kupreanof with his head.

Today, the town's economy is based on commercial fishing, fish processing and logging.

See also *Tlingit Indians & Totem Poles.*

◆ Kasegaluk Lagoon

Kasegaluk Lagoon, on the Chukchi Sea coast, is the largest barrier is-land-lagoon system in North America. The shallow (3-6 feet deep), 12-mile-long body of water offers excellent kayaking and wildlife viewing.

◆ Kashims

Kashims, or *kashgees*, are ceremonial houses still used by some Yup'ik Eskimos. Also known as "men's houses," kashims were traditionally built under the leadership of an elder man, and used by his male relatives as a gathering place in which to sleep, eat, work and socialize. The men's houses are often used for steambaths, as well.

See also *Eskimos.*

◆ Katalla

Today a ghost town, Katalla was an oil and coal boomtown just after the turn of the century. One of the first oil discoveries in Alaska was made near Katalla in 1896, near the mouth of the Katalla River southeast of Cordova. In 1902, the state's first oil well was drilled there by the Alaska Development Co. The media pounced on the news of an Alaska oil strike, greatly exaggerating the height of the gusher.

The remote town, established as a supply point, grew to a population of as many as 10,000 people. But, by 1910, after the government set re-strictions on coal mining and mineral development, the population had dwindled to 188. Between 1902 and 1931, a total of 36 wells were drilled in the Katalla oil field, 18 of which hit oil, but none of which resulted in a significant strike. A small refinery, built in 1911, supplied local markets with oil and gasoline until 1933, when the plant burned to the ground.

Katalla also has the distinction of being the location where the *Portland,* a coastal steamer which ran from Seattle to St. Michael at the mouth of the Yukon River, was wrecked in 1910. The ship had gained fame when it ar-rived in Seattle on July 17, 1897, with a ton-and-a-half of gold from the Klondike on board, helping set off one of the biggest gold rushes in history.

See also *Oil & Gold.*

◆ Katmai National Park and Preserve

In the Aleutian Range on the Alaska Peninsula, the violent eruption of Mt. Novarupta in 1912 caused Mt. Katmai to collapse and form the wondrous Valley of 10,000 Smokes—an area once covered by thousands of steam-spewing fumaroles (holes in volcanic areas from which steam and smoke escape). Only a few fumaroles are active today, and the crater has filled into a lake. Ash and pumice from the eruption also buried Ukak River under as much as 700 feet of debris; this area has been eroded by streams, which cut dramatic gorges through the waste.

Katmai National Park and Preserve's other claim to fame is its brown bears—the largest unhunted population in the world. The area is renowned for its sportfishing, including the red salmon runs in the Naknek River drainage that attract the bears. The forest and tundra lands abound with moose, caribou, red foxes, mink, marten and river otters; bald eagles nest throughout. Activities include canoeing, rafting, wildlife viewing, hiking and backpacking. In 1918, a national monument was created to preserve the Valley of 10,000 Smokes; in 1980 it was enlarged and became a national park and preserve, covering 4 million acres.

See also *National Parklands & Volcanoes.*

• Kayak

A kayak is a watertight Eskimo skin boat. Kayaks are made of wooden frames, which are completely covered with skins (such as walrus). Only one or two openings are left in the center for occupants, who use a double-bladed paddle to maneuver through the water. The modern-day kayak has the same basic structure as a traditional Eskimo kayak, but is built of wood or synthetic fibers.

See also *Bidarka; Boating, Canoeing, Kayaking and Rafting; & Umiak.*

• Kayak Island

Remote Kayak Island, in the Gulf of Alaska, was the site of the first documented landing of Europeans on North America's northwest coast. Naturalist Georg Wilhelm Steller and other members of an expedition led by Russian Capt. Cmdr. Vitus Bering landed near the mouth of a creek on the west shore of Kayak Island on July 20, 1741. Although ashore just a few hours to replenish water supplies, Steller sketched many plants and animals, including the Steller's jay (later named after him). No trace of their landing remains today, but the site is on the National Register of Historic Places. The narrow, 22-mile-long island is difficult to reach and often has stormy weather conditions.

See also *Vitus Bering & Georg Wilhelm Steller.*

◆ Della Keats

Della "Puyuk" Keats was an Inuit healer who combined modern medicinal techniques with the ancient skills of her people in her roles as tribal doctor and midwife. She held an honorary degree of Doctor of Human Letters in Health Sciences from the University of Alaska Anchorage. She died in 1986 in Kotzebue.

◆ Kenai

Kenai (pop. 6,613), named "All America City" in 1992, is the largest city on the Kenai Peninsula. Originally a Dena'ina Indian village, in 1791 it became the second permanent settlement established by the Russians in Alaska. In 1869 the U.S. Army established Fort Kenai (Kenay), and in 1899 a post office was authorized.

Oil exploration began in the mid-1950s. The Swanson River oil reserves were discovered in 1957, and natural gas was discovered in the Kalifornsky Beach area two years later. Cook Inlet's middle-ground shoals are believed to contain one of the major oil and gas fields in the world. Next to oil, tourism, fishing and fish processing are the leading industries.

◆ Kenai Fjords National Park

On the east coast of the Kenai Peninsula, the 669,000-acre Kenai Fjords National Park contains 700-square-mile Harding Icefield and a dramatic coastal mountain-fjord system. Substantial populations of marine mammals inhabit or migrate through the park's coastal waters, including sea otters, harbor seals, Steller sea lions, Dall porpoises and whales (minke, gray, fin, humpback). Thousands of sea birds, including puffins, kittiwakes, murres and auklets, are also found here. Day cruises to see the wildlife and tidewater glaciers are available out of Seward. Exit Glacier, connected by road to the Seward Highway, is the most accessible of the park's glaciers.

See also *National Parklands.*

◆ Kenai Peninsula

Located in Southcentral Alaska, the Kenai Peninsula (referred to as "the Kenai" by Alaskans) is bounded on the east by the Gulf of Alaska and Prince William Sound, and on the west by Cook Inlet. The Sterling and Seward highways access the Kenai Peninsula and its major communities:

Homer, Seward, Soldotna and Kenai.

The Kenai is a popular recreation area, both because of its proximity to Anchorage and its natural attractions. The 2-million-acre Kenai National Wildlife Refuge, along with Chugach National Forest, Kenai Fjords National Park and Kachemak Bay State Park, account for much of the total land area of the peninsula. Recreational activites include sportfishing, hiking, camping, hunting and river rafting.

See also *Homer, Kenai, Seward & Soldotna.*

◆ Kennecott Copper Mine

Located approximately 65 miles east of Chitina in the Wrangell–St. Elias Mountains, the Kennecott Copper Mine was the richest copper mine in the world until its closure. It was built between 1910 and 1920 by the Kennecott Copper Corp. Kennecott's mill processed more than 591,535 tons of copper ore and employed some 800 workers in its heyday. The workers lived in the mining town of Kennicott at the mine site. (An early-day misspelling resulted in the mining company being named Kennecott, while the region, river and settlement were known as Kennicott.)

Today, Kennicott is a ghost town in the Wrangell–St. Elias Mountains. When economic conditions forced the mine to shut down abruptly in 1938, the mine buildings were locked up and left as they were: utensils were left in kitchen drawers; maps, charts and records were left in offices; and surgical instruments were left in the infirmary. About 3 dozen of the original mine buildings remain, although the distinctive barn-red structures have deteriorated. Today, a lodge is located here. The museum in nearby McCarthy has historic photos and artifacts from the Kennecott Copper Mine.

◆ Ketchikan

Ketchikan (pop. 8,263), on Revillagigedo (ruh-vee-uh-guh-GAY-do) Island in Southeast Alaska, is Alaska's southernmost city and first port of call. The name Ketchikan is derived from the Tlingit name *Kitschk-Hin,* meaning the creek of the "thundering wings of an eagle."

Originally a Tlingit fish camp, white settlement began with establishment of a salmon cannery in 1886, followed by mining in the 1890s. Mining waned, but the salmon canneries boomed in the 1930s, and Ketchikan became the "Salmon Capital of the World." When salmon declined, the timber industry moved in. Today, tourism is a major industry here.

Ketchikan is Alaska's fifth-largest city, after Anchorage, Fairbanks, Juneau and Sitka. The town is centered around the waterfront on Tongass Narrows, with much of the business district built above the water on pilings. Major attractions include Creek Street (a former redlight district) and totem poles. Ketchikan's totems, located at the Totem Heritage Cultural Center (with 33 totems, Alaska's largest collection of original totems), Saxman Totem Park (26 totems) and Totem Bight, are one of the most-visited attractions in the state. The University of Alaska Southeast campus is located in Ketchikan.

◆ King Cove

King Cove (pop. 451), located on the Pacific Ocean side of the Alaska Peninsula, almost doubles its population during fishing season. The town was established in 1911, when Pacific-American Fisheries built a salmon cannery here. The cannery, which burned down and was then rebuilt in 1976, is the largest Alaska cannery operating under one roof. King Cove is also a port of call on the Alaska Marine Highway's Southcentral/Southwest ferry system.

◆ King Island

Located on Bering Strait, 45 miles off the west coast of Alaska, King Island is the ancestral home of the Ugiuvangmiut Eskimos. Most residents moved to Nome in the 1950s, and the island is now uninhabited except in May and June, when King Islanders return to gather bird eggs and hunt walrus.

◆ The Kink

The Kink, originally the name of a sharp bend in the North Fork Fortymile River, came to mean the 15-foot-wide channel that was blasted 100 feet through a ridge in the neck of the river in 1904. Engineers diverted the flow of the river, opening almost three miles of the riverbed to mining. The project was considered a major engineering feat at the time, though mining prospects turned out to be unprofitable. Today, the Kink

is on the National Register of Historic Places—a monument to man's un-
dertakings in the pursuit of gold at the turn of the century.

See also *Gold & Mining.*

◆ Kiska Island

During World War II, Kiska Island, in the western end of the Aleutian
chain, was invaded by the Japanese on June 7, 1942. Attu Island was also
occupied as the Japanese expanded their military hold in the Pacific. This
Japanese advance onto U.S. soil greatly alarmed America, provoking the
hurried building of the Alaska-Canada Military Highway (the Alaska Highway), which would allow the United States and Canada to mobilize troops
and equipment overland to Alaska.

Meanwhile, the Japanese constructed coastal and anti-aircraft defenses,
as well as camps, roads, an airfield and submarine base on Kiska. Allied
forces prepared to invade the island, but the Japanese secretly evacuated
under the cover of fog on July 28, 1943. When 34,000 U.S. and Canadian
troops arrived on Aug. 15, they didn't realize the island was deserted. In
dense fog, the allied troops shot at each other, killing 25 men and injuring
31. Allied camps were set up for the remainder of the war, and subsequently abandoned. Today, Kiska—unoccupied and strewn with debris from
wartime activity—is part of the Alaska Maritime National Wildlife Refuge.

See also *Alaska Highway, Attu Island & World War II.*

◆ Klondike Gold Rush National Historical Park

Established in 1976, Klondike Gold Rush National Historical Park is
actually four parks in one. Commemorating the great Klondike gold rush
of 1897-98, the park includes a six-block historic district in Skagway, the
townsite of Dyea, the Chilkoot and White Pass trails, and an interpretive
visitor center in Seattle (explaining Seattle's role as a jumping-off point for
prospectors during the Klondike gold rush). For further information, contact the Skagway Convention and Visitors Bureau (address and phone
number in For More Information section).

See also *Chilkoot Trail, Gold, National Parklands & Skagway.*

◆ Knik

Knik is referred to as the "Dog Mushing Center of the World" because
many famous mushers live in the area, including Joe Redington Sr., the

"father" of the Iditarod Trail race. The Knik Museum and the Sled Dog Mushers Hall of Fame contain regional memorabilia, a Canine Hall of Fame, and historic displays on the Iditarod Trail and Alaska mushers. Knik is a checkpoint on the annual Iditarod Trail Sled Dog Race. Originally a Tanaina Indian village, it is found on the west bank of Knik Arm in Cook Inlet, just northeast of Anchorage.

See also *Dog Mushing & Iditarod Trail Sled Dog Race.*

◆ Kobuk Valley National Park

Kobuk Valley National Park, a 1.7-million-acre area lying north of the Arctic Circle, has a diverse blend of biological, geological and cultural resources. Its most well-known features are the Great Kobuk Sand Dunes and Onion Portage.

The Kobuk Sand Dunes, which originated from glacial silt, make up the largest active dune field in the Arctic. Some of the dunes are as high as 100 feet, and summer temperatures among the shifting sands may be 90°F.

Onion Portage, on the Kobuk River, is one of the Arctic's most significant archeological sites. Humans have occupied the area for more than 12,000 years, hunting caribou as they cross the Kobuk River during seasonal migrations. Today, Eskimos continue to hunt the great herds.

Kobuk Valley's cold and dry climate is similar to that of the Ice Age. Its plant life resembles the flora of late Pleistocene times. During this period, the Kobuk Valley provided an ice-free corridor adjoining the Bering Land Bridge, which periodically formed between Alaska and Siberia.

Established in 1980, the park supports much wildlife, including a variety of mammals and more than 100 bird species. Activities include river running, hiking, canoeing, kayaking and fishing.

See also *Archeology, Eskimos & National Parklands.*

◆ Kodiak Island

Kodiak Island, in the Gulf of Alaska, is home to the oldest permanent European settlement in Alaska. Kodiak also houses the oldest parish in Alaska, a Russian Orthodox church built in 1794.

Known as "the Emerald Isle," Kodiak is the largest island in Alaska (3,670 square miles). It was first discovered by Stephen Glotov, a Russian explorer, in 1763. Alexander Baranof, manager of the Russian-America Co., used it as his headquarters, and Kodiak became Russian Alaska's first capital city, until the capital was moved to Sitka in 1804.

Other events in Kodiak's past include the eruption of Mt. Novarupta (on nearby Alaska Peninsula) in 1912, which covered the island with a black cloud of ash, and a tidal wave in 1964 caused by the Good Friday Earthquake, which destroyed the downtown area—including a fishing fleet, processing plants, canneries and more than 150 homes. During World War II, 25,000 American troops were positioned on the island at Fort Abercrombie.

The city of Kodiak (pop. 6,365), the largest city on Kodiak Island, is largely a fishing community. The Baranof Museum, or Erskine House, contains many historic items detailing the area's past, displayed in a warehouse built by the Russian-American Co. in 1808. The building was sold to W.J. Erskine in 1911, who converted it into a residence for a time; it was then referred to as the Erskine House. In 1962 it was declared a national historic landmark.

The Coast Guard occupies the old Kodiak Naval Station, and Fort Abercrombie is now a state park and national historic landmark. The Kodiak National Wildlife Refuge encompasses 1,865,000 acres on Kodiak, Uganik and Afognak islands. More than 2,500 bears are estimated to live on Kodiak Island.

See also *Fishing, Good Friday Earthquake, Islands, Russian-American Co., Russian Orthodox Church & Volcanoes.*

◆ Kotzebue

Kotzebue (pop. 2,751) is located just above the Arctic Circle on a 3-mile-long spit in Kotzebue Sound—a site that has been occupied for some 600 years. The population is predominantly Eskimo and the economy is based on commercial fishing, government services, subsistence hunting and fishing and reindeer herding. The town is also a supply point for communities in the sparsely populated northwestern area of Alaska. The NANA Museum of the Arctic in Kotzebue has exhibits on ethnology, natural history and wildlife of the region.

Outside town on the treeless tundra, someone planted a single white spruce about 20 years ago. With some nurturing it survived, and earned the facetious title, "Kotzebue National Forest." However, in the spring of 1993, a vandal chopped down the "forest."

◆ Kotzebue Sound

Kotzebue Sound, a part of the Chukchi Sea, lies on the Arctic Circle between the Bering Land Bridge National Preserve on Seward Peninsula and Cape Krusenstern National Park and Preserve on the mainland to the north. The 35-mile-wide, 80-mile-long sound was named by Russian Lt. Otto von Kotzebue (for himself) after he discovered the bay in 1816. Kotzebue had commanded two other round-the-world voyages; on the second one he explored the northwest coast of Alaska in search of the Northwest Passage.

See also *Northwest Passage.*

◆ Chief Kowee

An Auk Indian who lived on Admiralty Island, Chief Kowee is often credited with the 1880 discovery of gold in the Juneau area, rather than Joe Juneau and Richard Harris, the two prospectors mentioned in most accounts. It was Kowee who originally brought the ore sample to the attention of entrepreneur George Pilz, hoping to bring prosperity to his people. Pilz then grubstaked Juneau and Harris to locate the source. The pair returned empty handed, and Kowee then led them up Gold Creek to the source.

◆ Kuspuk

A kuspuk is an Eskimo woman's garment—a hooded, cloth parka covered with a brightly colored print. Kuspuks are also worn as dresses or light jackets during summer.

Frank Whaley Photo

◆ Kwethluk

Kwethluk (pop. 558) gained a name for itself in 1890 when an Eskimo lay missionary of the Moravian church was murdered by the men of Kwethluk and his body left to be eaten by dogs. J.H. Kilbuck, another missionary, had arrived at the town after hearing reports that the first man may have gone insane, but the Natives forced Kilbuck to leave a few days before the man was killed.

After the turn of the century, Kwethluk developed into a small gold-prospecting community, based around some mostly unsuccessful placer mines on the Kwethluk River. One deposit at Canyon Creek was mined until World War II.

◆ Lake Clark National Park and Preserve

Across Cook Inlet from Kenai Peninsula, north of Iliamna Lake, Lake Clark National Park and Preserve offers a diverse show of geological features. Located at the convergence of the Alaska and Aleutian mountain ranges, the park and preserve includes the 50-mile-long Lake Clark; two active volcanoes—Mt. Iliamna (10,016 feet) and Mt. Redoubt (10,197 feet); three national 'wild rivers—Chilikadrotna, Mulchatna and Tlikakila; a rocky coastline along Cook Inlet; and countless glaciers. The terrain varies from coastal lowlands of spruce trees and marshes to alpine meadows and lichen-covered uplands.

Established in 1980, the park and preserve cover 3.6 million acres. Wildlife includes brown and black bears, caribou, moose, Dall sheep, wolves, wolverines and red foxes. Recreational activities include backpacking, river running and fishing.

See also *Glaciers, National Parklands & Volcanoes.*

◆ Lakes

Alaska has millions of lakes, 94 of which have a surface area of more than 10 square miles. The largest lakes in Alaska are Iliamna (1,000 square miles), Becharof (458), Teshekpuk (315), Naknek (242) and Tustumena (117). Three of these—Iliamna, Becharof and Naknek—are on the Alaska Peninsula, while Lake Clark is just to the north of it.

See also *Becharof Lake, Iliamna Lake & Lake Clark National Park and Preserve.*

✦ Land

See *Alaska, Alaska National Interest Lands Conservation Act, Alaska Native Claims Settlement Act, D-2 Lands, Homesteading & National Parklands.*

✦ Languages

Many Native languages are still spoken in Alaska's Native communities, though most Natives are bilingual in English and their own language. Native languages include Aleut, Yupik, Inupiaq, Haida, Tlingit, Tsimshian, Eyak and many Athabascan languages (including Ahtna, Tanaina, Inglaik, Holikachuk, Koyukon, Upper Kuskokwim, Tanana, Tanacross, Upper Tanana, Han and Kutchin).

See also *Natives.*

✦ Sydney Lawrence

Sydney Lawrence (1865-1940), Alaska's most renowned resident artist, arrived in Juneau in 1903, inspired, like thousands of other men and women, by the pursuit of gold. Lawrence had lived, studied and painted in New York, Paris, Venice, Cornwall and North Africa. After nine years of prospecting in Valdez, he became intrigued by Mt. McKinley/Denali—the highest peak on the continent—and decided to paint it. Less than a year later, he had finished 40 oil sketches of the peak.

In 1914, two of his large canvases, *Top of the Continent* and *The Trapper*, were exhibited in the Smithsonian Institute in Washington, DC. The resulting national exposure and demand for his work allowed Lawrence to support himself solely by painting. He worked in the growing town of Anchorage until 1925. At that time, Lawrence moved to Los Angeles for health reasons, but he continued to visit and paint Alaska.

✦ Lichen

Lichen, the earth's longest-living plant, is perhaps the most important vegetation in Alaska. Composed of two organisms living symbiotically—an alga and a fungus—lichen is an important food for reindeer and caribou, especially in winter. Humans and dogs are also able to rely on lichen as a survival food when other food sources become unavailable. Lichen grows on rocks or bark and is among the first growth to appear in silt left by retreating glaciers.

See also *Caribou, Glaciers, Reindeer & Vegetation.*

◆ Little Diomede Island

See *Diomede Islands.*

◆ Livengood

In July 1914, Nathaniel R. Hudson and Jay Livengood discovered gold on a creek 50 miles northwest of Fairbanks. By 1920, the mining camp sluiced out $9.5 million in gold. During the 1930s and '40s, large-scale mining was attempted with little success, and Livengood became a ghost town. However, with the building of the trans-Alaska pipeline and the North Slope Haul Road during the '70s, Livengood was revived. In 1977, a gold mining corporation bought much of the gold-rich Livengood Bench. Today, about 100 people live in the area.

See also *Gold, Mining & Trans-Alaska Pipeline.*

◆ Lower 48

Many Alaskans refer to the 48 contiguous American states as the Lower 48.

See also *Outside.*

◆ Lynx

Lynx are found throughout Alaska, except for the southern Alaska Peninsula and the Yukon-Kuskokwim Delta. They prey primarily on the snowshoe hare. Lynx are shy, nocturnal animals; few people sight them in the wild. They have a light brown or grayish coat and short, black-tipped tail. Equipped with large feet, they maneuver easily over deep snow. Lynx weigh up to 45 pounds.

See also *Hares.*

M

✦ Malaspina Glacier

Malaspina Glacier is the largest glacier in North America. Originating in the St. Elias Mountains, it covers about 850 square miles, terminating between Yakutat Bay and Icy Bay in Southeast. Malaspina Glacier is about one-third larger than Alaska's second-largest glacier—Bering. However, the Bering system with all of its tributary glaciers covers 200 more square miles than the Malaspina system.

In 1874, William H. Dall named the glacier Malaspina Plateau—mistaking it for land because it was covered with moraine (glacial sediment). Six years later it was discovered to be a glacier. Its namesake is the Italian explorer, Capt. Don Alessandro Malaspina, who sailed the northwest coast of North America in 1791.

See also *Glaciers*.

✦ Mammals

More than 90 species of mammals are found in Alaska, including 12 species of big game and 19 species of furbearers. Some species, such as the musk ox and polar bear, are extremely rare or do not exist in other parts of the United States.

See *Bison, Caribou, Dall Sheep, Deer, Dolphins and Porpoises, Elk, Foxes, Hares, Lynx, Moose, Mountain Goats, Musk Oxen, Otters, Collared Pikas, Sea Lions, Seals, Squirrels, Walrus, Weasels, Whales & Wolves.*

◆ Marine Life

See *Dolphins and Porpoises, Otters, Sea Lions, Seals, Walrus & Whales.*

◆ Marmot

See *Squirrels.*

◆ Masks

Ceremonial masks are intrinsic to the culture of Alaska's Eskimo, Aleut and coastal Indian people. Worn by ceremonial dancers and shaman into the early 20th century, mask-making continues today as a modern art.

Traditional Eskimo masks were made from driftwood. Modern innovations include miniature ivory masks, whalebone masks and caribou skin masks. Aleut masks often had attachments of wood and were painted or decorated with feathers. Cedar and alder masks with colorful, highly stylized totemic designs are part of the Native tradition of Southeast Alaska's Tlingit and other coastal Indians.

Another type of headgear prized by the Eskimo and Aleut people was that of visors made of wood or skin, and bentwood hats, both of which were worn by hunters and warriors. The hats and visors were extremely valued possessions, indicative of the high status of those who wore them.

◆ Massacre Bay

See *Attu Island.*

◆ Matanuska Glacier

In 1979, part of Matanuska Glacier flowed more than 100 feet in two-months' time. Scientists are unsure of the cause of this rapid advance.

The 27-mile-long glacier heads in the Chugach Mountains northwest of Anchorage. Matanuska's average width is 2 miles, and its terminus is 4 miles wide. The glacier can be seen from the Glenn Highway. Access to the foot of the Matanuska Glacier is across private land.

The glacier was named in 1898 for the Matanuska River. (The word "Matanuska" derived from the Russian *Matanooski*, meaning "copper river people"—the Russian name for the Ahtna Indians on the Copper River.)

See also *Glaciers.*

• Matanuska Valley Colony

In 1934, during the Great Depression, President Franklin Delano Roosevelt's Federal Emergency Relief Administration began a unique program to help employ Midwest farmers: the Matanuska Valley Colony. Social workers picked 203 families from the states of Minnesota, Michigan and Wisconsin to relocate and set up farms in Alaska. The federal government provided transportation, equipment, land and buildings.

The Matanuska Valley was chosen for its relatively good climate, soils and railroad access. Although the project was plagued by disorganization on the government's part and the farmers' inexperience in dealing with the Alaska climate, the project had moderate success and descendants of some of the original farmers still live in the area today.

See also *Agriculture & Palmer.*

• Mat-Su

The term Mat-Su is commonly used to refer to the collective Matanuska and Susitna river valleys, Alaska's prime agricultural region.

See also *Agriculture.*

• McGrath

In February 1924, McGrath (pop. 528) became the first Alaska town to receive mail by air. It was delivered by pioneer aviator Carl Ben Eielson. McGrath developed as a supply point for the Kuskokwim and Innoko river valleys as prospecting became more popular in the late 1800s. Today, it continues as a supply and transportation center for the Upper Kuskokwim region.

See also *Carl Ben Eielson.*

• McNeil River

The McNeil River State Game Sanctuary draws photographers and wildlife buffs from around the world with its large number of brown bears that arrive to feed on spawning chum salmon. As many as 60 bears may feed at the same time during peak season (June through August). The 22-mile river is bordered to the south by the Katmai National Park and Preserve and empties into Kamishak Bay at the base of the Alaska Peninsula. It was named earlier this century for area rancher Charlie McNeil.

There are no visitor facilities at the McNeil River sanctuary. Visitors must be prepared for a true wilderness experience, and a special bear-viewing permit is required to visit during peak season. For further information contact the Alaska Department of Fish and Game (address and phone in For More Information section).

See also *Bears.*

◆ Mendenhall Glacier

Mendenhall Glacier, one of the most visited sights in Alaska, terminates fewer than 15 miles away from Juneau. The 12-mile-long glacier ends in Mendenhall Lake—a 200-foot-deep freshwater reservoir formed in the early part of this century, which continues to enlarge as the glacier retreats. Mendenhall is one of many glaciers that drain the Juneau Icefield. It is named for Thomas Corwin Mendenhall (1841-1924), a former superintendent of the U.S. Coast and Geodetic Survey.

See also *Glaciers & Juneau Icefield.*

◆ Metlakatla

See *Tsimshian Indians.*

◆ Military Bases

Alaska's strategic military position was recognized at the beginning of World War II. After the start of the war, the Japanese invasion of the Aleutian Islands prompted an immediate defensive reaction by the United States, leading to the construction of the Alaska Highway and the permanent installation of the military in Alaska. Because of its proximity to the Soviet Union, Alaska remained in the forefront of North American defensive strategies during the Cold War years, as well.

Today, the military is centered around bases in Anchorage and Fairbanks. Near Fairbanks, the Army has Forts Wainwright and Greely; and outside of Anchorage is Fort Richardson Army Base. The Air Force has two large bases: Eielson Air Force Base near Fairbanks and Elmendorf Air Force Base in Anchorage. Eielson was named for the pioneer aviator and bush pilot, Carl Ben Eielson.

Other military installations include the Army National Guard and Air National Guard in Anchorage; the Coast Guard headquarters in Juneau; and Navy and Marine Corps commands and detachments in Anchorage at Elmendorf. Air Force installations at Shemya Island, King Salmon and Galena have closed, as has the Navy station on Adak Island.

◆ Mining

Metals and minerals mined in Alaska range from aluminum to zinc, although fluctuating prices on the world market determine much of the mining activity in the state. Principal minerals mined in Alaska are zinc, gold, silver, lead, tin and platinum, which account for more than 80 percent of the state's total production. Zinc is the most valuable commodity produced, and Alaska is the largest producer of zinc in the United States. Most of the zinc comes from the Red Dog Mine.

Of the 20 largest mining companies in Alaska (ranked by employees), most are mining for gold, which is the second most valuable mineral commodity produced in the state. Placer deposits account for most of Alaska's gold mining, although lode mines have produced significant amounts of gold. Treadwell Mine was the earliest major gold mining operation in Alaska and one of the world's largest underground gold mines. Located across the channel from Juneau on Douglas Island, Treadwell operated from 1884 to 1922, although a disastrous cave-in in 1917 closed three of its four mines.

The Green's Creek Mine on Admiralty Island is the largest silver mine in North America. Silver is most often recovered as a by-product of copper mining, an industry that began in Alaska around the turn of the century. The Kennecott Mine in the Wrangell Mountains, abandoned in 1938, is Alaska's most famous copper mine.

Other mineral products mined in Alaska include coal, lead, molybdenum, platinum, sand and gravel, and marble. Sand and gravel ranks behind oil and gas in value. Most of the state's coal is mined at the Usibelli Coal Mine near Healy, of which half is used in Interior Alaska, and half exported to South Korea. Marble was quarried at Tokeen on Marble Island in Southeast Alaska from 1902 to 1930, and provided marble for interior work on dozens of public buildings in the Lower 48, as well as the state Capitol Building in Juneau.

See also *Alaska-Juneau Mine, Gold, Kennecott Copper Mine, Oil & Red Devil.*

◆ Mink

See *Weasels*.

◆ Misty Fiords National Monument

Misty Fiords National Monument, located 30 miles east of Ketchikan in Tongass National Forest, encompasses 2.3 million acres. It takes its name from the constant precipitation characteristic of its coastal rainforest environment and the myriad fjord-like inlets, bays, arms and coves that cut into the coastline. Waterfalls plunge to salt water along the steep-walled waterways, fed by lakes and streams that absorb an annual rainfall in excess of 14 feet. Behm Canal, known for it extraordinary length (100 miles) and depth, cuts through the monument, and is a popular destination for cruise ships and kayakers alike.

Established in 1978, Misty Fiords is the largest wilderness area in Alaska's national forests, and the second largest in the U.S. National Forest system.

◆ Moose

Moose are the largest member of the deer family, and Alaska moose are the largest of their species, with males weighing up to 1,600 pounds. Moose range throughout Alaska, except in the Kodiak Island group and on islands in Southeast Alaska, Prince William Sound and the Bering Sea. Moose browse on willow, birch and aspen twigs, sedges, grasses and pond weeds. They are the most popular big game animal in Alaska. Unpredictable and aggressive, moose will charge humans and dogs.

◆ Mosquitoes

See *Insects*.

◆ Mount McKinley/Denali

The highest mountain in North America is the twin-peaked Mt. McKinley, also called Denali (Athabascan for the "Great One" or "the High One"). Located in the Alaska Range within Denali National Park, the mountain was named for President William McKinley in 1896 by W.A. Dickey, a prospector. Its two peaks are collectively referred to as the Churchill Peaks. (Nearby Mt. Foraker, 17,400 feet, is know as Memlale, or "Denali's Wife.")

McKinley's north peak (19,470 feet) was first climbed by the Sourdough Party in 1909. The higher south peak (20,320 feet) was first climbed in 1913 by the Hudson Stuck expedition. Joe Crosson made the first aiprlane landing on McKinley in April 1932, flying a Fairchild monoplane on skis. In 1947, Barbara Washburn became the first woman to reach the summit, climbing the south and north peaks on successive days. She was accompanied by her husband, Bradford Washburn, who was to pioneer the West Buttress route in 1951. The first solo ascent was made in August 1970, by Japanese climber Naomi Uemura. In 1984, Uemura made the first winter solo ascent, but he disappeared on the descent from the summit during a storm.

See also *Denali National Park & Hudson Stuck.*

◆ Mountain Goats

Mountain goats are found in mountains throughout Southeast and in the coastal mountains of Southcentral, and have been transplanted to Kodiak and Baranof islands. Mountain goats have white coats, a long beard, black muzzle, pointed ears and a sturdy body. They generally weigh between 150 and 300 pounds. Mountains goats are distinguished from the all-white Dall sheep by their black horns. The male's horns are curved and may grow to one foot in length. The female's horns are shorter. With just one offspring per year, mountain goats are slow to recover from overhunting or harsh winters. They are one of the most challenging of game animals; hunters must follow them over steep and treacherous terrain.

◆ Mountaineering

Each year, thousands of mountain climbers head to Alaska to attempt its challenging peaks. About 1,000 climbers a year try Mt. McKinley/Denali.

The number of climbers on McKinley/Denali has tripled since the 1970s. An average of two fatalities occur each year on the mountain. In 1967, seven climbers were killed on McKinley/Denali; in 1992, 11 died.

Other climbers head for Alaska's lesser known and often more difficult peaks, including ice climbs on Mt. Hunter (14,573 feet) and Mt. Huntington (12,240) in the Alaska Range, and the solitude and drier climate of peaks in the northern Brooks Range. Mt. St. Elias, the second-highest mountain in Alaska, is also popular with mountaineers. For further information on mountain climbing, consult *The ALASKA WILDERNESS GUIDE*, available from Vernon Publications. Also, contact the Alaska Public Lands Information Center (addresses and phone numbers in For More Information section).

See also *Mountains.*

◆ Mountains

The three highest mountain peaks in the United States are in Alaska: Mt. McKinley/Denali, South Peak (20,320 feet); Mt. McKinley/Denali, North Peak (19,470); and Mt. St. Elias (18,008). Other major peaks include Mounts Foraker (17,400), Blackburn (16,523), Bona (16,421) and Sanford (16,237). Alaska has 19 peaks over 14,000 feet.

The longest mountain ranges in the state are the Brooks and Alaska ranges. The Brooks Range, in the north, separates the Arctic from the Interior region. The Alaska Range forms a barrier between the Interior and the southcentral and southeast areas. The Aleutian Range, which extends in a southwesterly direction from the Alaska Range, continues into the Pacific Ocean as the Aleutian Island chain. Shorter mountain ranges in Alaska include the Chugach, Wrangell, St. Elias and Kuskokwim mountains.

See also *Alaska Range, Aleutian Range, Brooks Range, Chugach Mountains, Coast Mountains, Mountaineering, St. Elias Range, Volcanoes & Wrangell-St. Elias National Park and Preserve.*

◆ Movies

In 1982, the state of Alaska formed the Alaska Film Office (one of a variety of ways the state is working to diversify its economy as oil revenues decline). As a division of the Office of Tourism, the film office works to increase revenues from filmmaking in Alaska, promoting the state as a viable place to set films. In the past, most films set in Alaska were actually filmed on sound stages or in snowy locations closer to Hollywood.

Recent movies filmed in Alaska include *Runaway Train* (1985), filmed along stretches of Alaska Railroad tracks; *White Fang* (1990), shot in Haines; and *Salmonberries* (1990), an independent film starring k.d. lang, shot in Kotzebue. Parts of other feature films have been filmed on location in Alaska, such as a scene with Capt. Kirk and Dr. McCoy in *Star Trek VI: The Undiscovered Country* (1991), shot on Knik Glacier, a short distance from Anchorage; part of *Never Cry Wolf* (1983), in which a caribou stampede was done with domestic reindeer herds near Nome; and *The Hunt for Red October* (1989), in which a scene in an icy "Russian" fjord was actually filmed in Resurrection Bay near Seward.

◆ Mukluks

Mukluks are soft, Eskimo boots made of animal skin and fur. They are designed and insulated for cold-weather wear. Some modern-day takeoffs on mukluks are made of other fibers, such as wool.

◆ Muktuk

Muktuk—an Eskimo delicacy—consists of the skin and attached blubber of a whale. Muktuk is usually eaten raw, although sometimes it is dried or cooked. The snack is high in nutrients and fat, both of which are essential to survival in the Arctic.

◆ Museums

Alaska has a variety of museums with displays and information on topics such as fossils, sled dogs, totem poles, mining artifacts and many other aspects of the state's history and resources. The Anchorage Museum of History and Art and the University of Alaska Museum in Fairbanks both rank in the 10 most-visited attractions in Alaska.

Other museums include the Alaska State Museum in Juneau, the Carrie McLain Memorial Museum in Nome, the Cordova Historical Museum, the Juneau Douglas City Museum, the Oscar Anderson House Museum in Anchorage, the Samuel K. Fox Museum in Dillingham, the Sheldon Jackson Museum in Sitka, the State of Alaska Railroad Museum in Nenana, the Tongass Historical Museum in Ketchikan, the Totem Heritage Center in Ketchikan, the Trail of '98 City Museum in Skagway, the Valdez Museum, the Wales Museum and the Wrangell Museum.

For further information contact the Alaska Division of Tourism, the Anchorage Museum of History and Art or the University of Alaska Museum (addresses and phone numbers in For More Information section).

✦ Muskeg

Muskeg is the grassy bog or swamp land that covers much of the state of Alaska. Underlying permafrost keeps muskeg from draining. The swampy ground is caused by an accumulation of moss, leaves and decayed plant matter. During summer it is soft and grassy, while during the winter it freezes solid.

See also *Permafrost.*

✦ Musk Oxen

By 1865, musk oxen had been hunted to extinction in Alaska. However, in 1935, the U.S. government allocated $40,000 to purchase 34 musk oxen from Greenland for reintroduction to the state. These animals were first hosted by the University of Alaska at Fairbanks, and five years later musk oxen were placed on Nunivak Island—a windy, treeless and predator-free habitat. By 1968, the herd had increased to 750. Since then, surplus animals have been moved to other areas, such as Unalakleet and the Seward Peninsula. Today, qiviut—the soft, underhair of the musk ox—supports a small manufacturing industry.

Musk oxen have big shoulder humps and swayed backs, but their long shaggy fur masks their body from full view. A bull may weigh close to 900 pounds. Eskimos call musk ox *umingmak,* "the bearded one."

See also *Qiviut.*

✦ Muskrats

Muskrats are found throughout most of mainland Alaska, except for the Arctic region. These large rodents, with dark brown pelts, are very active around breakup, when melting ice destroys their winter homes and males head out to seek mates. Although their pelts are worth little individually, the volume of furs taken during their springtime activity is one of the greatest of any species in Alaska.

◆ Naknek

The town of Naknek (pop. 575), near the mouth of the Naknek River on the Alaska Peninsula, is the seat of the state's oldest borough—Bristol Bay, incorporated in 1962. The region was settled more than 6,000 years ago by Yup'ik Eskimos and Athabascan Indians. In the 19th century, the Russians built a fort near the present townsite, and fur trappers inhabited the area. Historical attractions in Naknek are the Bristol Bay Historical Museum and the Russian Orthodox St. John the Baptist Chapel.

When the first salmon cannery opened in Bristol Bay in 1883, Naknek developed as a fishing and fish processing center for the region. Today, the town's population quadruples each summer as seasonal employees arrive to work on fishing boats and in the canneries. The Naknek River system supports five species of salmon and is a well-known sportfishing destination.

Northern Consolidated Airlines

✦ National Forests

See *Chugach National Forest & Tongass National Forest.*

✦ National Parklands

Two-thirds (54.7 million acres) of the total acreage of national parks in America (about 80.7 million acres) is located in Alaska. These lands fall into one of three categories: parks or monuments, which contain a number of significant natural resources and enough surrounding land to protect them; preserves, which are similar to parks and monuments, but may allow sport hunting and trapping and the extraction of minerals and fuels; and historical parks, which preserve and commemorate places of national historic importance.

Alaska has 15 national parks, the first of which was established in 1910 at Sitka, and the most recent of which was added in 1976 (the Klondike Gold Rush National Historical Park). Many well-known landmarks, such as Mt. McKinley/Denali and Glacier Bay, are preserved in national parklands, as well as lesser-known wonders such as the Grand Canyon of the Noatak in Noatak National Preserve. In 1980, the Alaska National Interest Lands Conservation Act (ANILCA) established 10 new national parklands in Alaska, and expanded three existing parks (Glacier Bay, Katmai and Denali). This act alone more than doubled the size of America's national park system.

For further information on Alaska's national parklands, contact the Alaska Public Lands Information Center (address and phone in For More Information section).

See also *Alaska National Interest Lands Conservation Act, Aniakchak National Monument and Preserve, Bering Land Bridge National Preserve, Cape Krusenstern National Monument, Denali National Park, Gates of the Arctic National Park and Preserve, Glacier Bay National Park and Preserve, Katmai National Park and Preserve, Kenai Fjords National Park, Klondike Gold Rush National Historical Park, Kobuk Valley National Park, Lake Clark National Park and Preserve, Noatak National Preserve, Sitka National Historical Park, Wrangell-St. Elias National Park and Preserve & Yukon-Charley Rivers National Preserve.*

✦ National Wildlife Refuges and Ranges

Alaska's wildlife refuges make up 88 percent of all lands in the National Wildlife Refuge System. The purpose of these refuges is to protect natural habitats and wildlife; people are allowed to use refuge lands, but all use must be compatible with the preservation of wildlife.

In Alaska most refuges are difficult to reach, and nearly all are true wilderness—untouched or unaltered by humans. The first refuges in Alaska were established in the early 1900s to protect nesting seabirds.

The most important act of legislation affecting the refuges was the Alaska National Interest Lands Conservation Act of 1980. Seven refuges were increased in size and nine new ones created. The Lands Act doubled the size of the National Wildlife Refuge System, bringing it to more than 87 million acres. The largest in size is the Yukon Delta Refuge (19.6 million acres), while total refuge-system acreage in Alaska is more than 77 million acres.

For further information, contact the U.S. Fish and Wildlife Service (address and phone in For More Information section).

See also *Alaska National Interest Lands Conservation Act & Arctic National Wildlife Refuge.*

◆ Native Corporations

In 1971, with the Alaska Native Claims Settlement Act, a long-standing dispute over Native land rights was settled. The government awarded 44 million acres and $962.5 million to Alaska Natives, with the stipulation that the land and money be given to regional and village corporations, rather than to traditional Native groups or clans.

Twelve regional and 200 village corporations were formed. The corporations, which hold title to Native lands, are organized to be profit-making entities, and do not provide social services. (Many other non-profit associations work to address the needs of Alaska Natives.) Some Native corporations have been successful, while others have had serious financial problems. The 12 regional corporations are NANA Regional Corp., Arctic Slope Regional Corp., Doyon Ltd., Bering Straits Native Corp., Calista Corp., Bristol Bay Native Corp., The Aleut Corp., Koniag Corp., Cook Inlet Region Corp., Chugach Natives Inc., Ahtna Inc. and Sealaska Corp. A 13th corporation was later formed, representing Alaska Natives who live outside the state.

See also *Alaska Federation of Natives, Alaska Natives Claim Settlement Act & Natives.*

◆ Natives

When Europeans discovered Alaska in 1741, the land was populated by the indigenous Eskimo, Indian and Aleut peoples, all of whom had distinct and complex cultures. The Eskimos and Aleuts lived in the Far North, along the western coast of Alaska and in the Aleutian chain, and depended on the sea for their livelihood. The Athabascan Indians, in Interior Alaska, led a semi-nomadic life—following the seasonal migrations of caribou, waterfowl and other game. Tlingit and Haida Indians resided in permanent settlements in Southeast, an area with a plentiful food stock and milder climate.

The influx of Russians and other Europeans caused immediate and extensive damage to Alaska Natives, including the ravaging effects of diseases to which they had no immunity. During the 1800s, a number of Natives were forced into hunting and trapping for European traders, who were supplying Europe's tremendous demand for furs. The Eskimos, Aleuts and Athabascans had to make the transition to a cash economy, which greatly differed from their traditional subsistence methods.

By the 1950s, all Alaska Natives had settled in permanent locations; the last to give up a nomadic lifestyle were the Inupiat Eskimo hunters who settled at Anaktuvuk Pass. Most Native villages are in isolated locations in the Bush. Although a number of Natives now live in urban centers such as Anchorage and Fairbanks, many still return to help their kin with seasonal subsistence activities. For further information on visiting Native villages, consult *The ALASKA WILDERNESS GUIDE*, available from Vernon Publications.

See also *Alaska Native Brotherhood, Alaska Federation of Natives, Alaska Native Claims Settlement Act, Aleuts, Athabascans, Eskimos, Haida Indians, Native Corporations, Population, Subsistence, Tlingit Indians, Tsimshians, The Tundra Times & Tyonek.*

◆ Nenana

Nenana means "a good place to camp between rivers." The town of Nenana (pop. 393), at the confluence of the Tanana and Nenana rivers, began in 1902 with the establishment of a roadhouse and trading post. As a base camp for the Alaska Railroad, Nenana boomed during its construction. On July 15, 1923, a golden spike was driven at the north end of a 700-foot steel bridge over the Tanana River, signifying completion of the railroad; the tracks connect Nenana with Fairbanks and Anchorage. The Alaska Railroad Museum, which is on the National Register of Historic

Places, is housed in the original Nenana Railroad Depot, built in 1923 and renovated in 1988.

With the completion of the railroad, Nenana became a transportation hub, where goods were transferred from railroad cars to river barges to supply communities on the Tanana and Yukon rivers.

See also *Alaska Railroad & Nenana Ice Classic.*

◆ Nenana Ice Classic

The Nenana Ice Classic is an annual event in which cash prizes are awarded to contestants who guess the time of ice breakup on the Tanana River. The contest began in 1917 when some Alaska Railroad construction workers whiled away their winter boredom by selling tickets for guesses. The contest, held every year since its inception, has grown into a widely publicized event. Festivities begin each February, with the Tripod Raising Festival and Nenana Ice Classic Dog Race, and end in late April or May with breakup.

To determine the exact time of breakup, contest organizers set up a tripod on the river ice; when the first crack occurs, the surging ice dislodges the tripod. A line attached to the tripod breaks, stopping a clock, which records the official breakup time. The people who come closest to guessing the exact minute, hour and day win thousands of dollars. In recent years, close to 200,000 guesses have been sold.

See also *Breakup & Nenana.*

◆ Ninilchik

On Memorial Day weekend, the community of Ninilchik (pop. 456) is referred to as the third biggest city in Alaska as thousands of anglers arrive to fish the waters in and around Deep Creek. The area, including Deep Creek, the Ninilchik River and part of Cook Inlet, is renowned for its saltwater king salmon fishing and record-size halibut. Anglers also catch silver, red and pink salmon. A major halibut fishery off Ninilchik has produced some of the largest trophy halibut found in Cook Inlet, including a 466-pound unofficial world-record sport-caught halibut.

Ninilchik was established by the Russian-American Co. in 1820 and used as an agricultural settlement and fur trappers' base. From the original community—a short distance from present-day Ninilchik—a small, white church, a cemetery, a store building and a few log cabins remain. Ninilchik is an Indian word meaning, "not a bad-looking little place."

See also *Russian-American Co., Fishing & Salmon.*

*"The Master returned and reported that
he had found the Inlet or rather river
contracted to the breadth of one league
by low land on each side...All hopes of a
passage was now given up...If the
discovery of this River [Cook Inlet]
should prove of use, either to the present
or future ages, the time spent in exploring it ought to be the less regreted, but to
us who had a much greater object in view
it was an essential loss..."*

— *Captain James Cook
June 1, 1778*

◆ Noatak National Preserve

Established in 1910, the 6.6-million-acre Noatak National Preserve protects the entire watershed of the 396-mile-long Noatak River. Along its
course, the river has carved the striking 65-mile-long Grand Canyon of the
Noatak.

The broad, sloping river valley is one of the most spectacular and well-
preserved wilderness areas in the world. The terrain ranges from boreal forest to treeless tundra. Great herds of caribou seasonally cross the Noatak
River, going to and from their calving grounds. Other wildlife include moose,
brown bears, Dall sheep, beavers, wolves and foxes, and more than 125 bird
species. The wildlife, though abundant by arctic standards, is limited

by the slow-growing vegetation. The park offers a variety of river activities, backpacking and wildlife viewing.

See also *National Parklands.*

◆ Nome

In 1899, the gold rush town of Dawson City in Yukon Territory was still prospering when news came of a gold strike in Nome. By August 1900, an estimated 20,000 people had stampeded to the once-isolated community on the Seward Peninsula. That year, Nome was considered the largest city in Alaska. Three men—Jafet Lindeberg, Eric Lindblom and John Brynteson—who were among the first to stake claims on Anvil Creek near Nome, became instant millionaires. Thousands of miners staked claims and pitched tents along the Bering Sea coast. By 1906, after most of the easy gold was gone, the stampeders left to try their fortune elsewhere. Many abandoned dredges are still found along the coast at Nome.

Nome owes its current name to a misinterpretation of a manuscript chart prepared aboard the HMS *Herald*; the annotation read: "? name." In 1900, the chief cartographer of the British Admiralty explained the mistake, saying the "?" was taken as a "C" (for cape) and the "a" was thought to be an "o." Thus, "Cape Nome" was read, and the nearby town was named Nome. The original settlement was called Anvil City, after Anvil Creek, site of the first major gold strike.

Today, gold mining continues to be an important economic activity. Nome (pop. 3,500) is also a transportation and commerce center for northwestern Alaska. It functions as a jumping-off point for visits to Russia (an hour flight away) and is a major stopover on tours of the Arctic. Employment in Nome is largely government-based. Some other jobs are provided by the reindeer industry.

The Bering Sea is a stone's throw from Nome's main street. In 1951, the Army Corps of Engineers completed a granite sea wall—3,350 feet long and 65 feet wide at the base—protecting Nome from the sea.

The Carrie McLain Memorial Museum has a large collection of gold rush photos and displays on early Eskimo life, the Bering Land Bridge and dog mushing. Each March, Nome is the site of the finish line for the Iditarod Trail Sled Dog Race, which starts in Anchorage.

See also *Gold, Iditarod Trail Sled Dog Race & Reindeer.*

◆ The *Norge*

In 1926, the *Norge*, piloted by Roald Amundsen, became the first dirigible to be flown over the North Pole. Amundsen flew from Spitzbergen, Norway, and intended to land at Nome. Instead, bad weather forced him to land on May 13 on the beach at Teller. Today, the site is on the National Register of Historic Places, and a plaque has been placed on an old two-story, false-front building in Teller, which stored some disassembled parts and gear from the *Norge*.

◆ North Pole

Each year, the town of North Pole, AK receives a tremendous amount of mail from the U.S. Postal Service, accepted on behalf of one Mr. Claus—also known as Santa Claus. Although many a believer may look at this spot on the map with wonder, North Pole (pop. 1,456) was actually bought and subdivided by the Dahl and Gaske Development Co. in 1944. The company hoped to attract a toy manufacturer who could advertise its products as being made in North Pole.

Today, many residents commute to Fairbanks. A North Pole oil refinery produces heating fuel, jet fuel and other products, and the town is close to the Eielson and Wainwright military bases.

◆ North Slope

The North Slope is a region of northern Alaska between the Brooks Range and the Arctic Ocean. In 1968, great deposits of oil and natural gas were found on the Arctic shore of the North Slope in Prudhoe Bay, a discovery that resulted in the building of the 800-mile trans-Alaska pipeline and generated billions of dollars in revenue for the state of Alaska and private oil companies.

See also *Oil, Prudhoe Bay & Trans-Alaska Pipeline.*

◆ Northern Lights

See *Aurora Borealis.*

◆ Northway

Northway (area pop. 364) is an important port of entry for air traffic to Alaska. Northway's airport was built in the 1940s as part of the Northwest Staging Route, a chain of air bases between Edmonton, AB, and Fairbanks.

Historically, the Northway area was occupied by the Athabascan Indians, whose traditions and culture continue today. Northway was named for an Athabascan chief who had adopted the name of a riverboat captain in the early 1900s.

The community is located within Tetlin National Wildlife Refuge. The 950,000-acre refuge, known for its high density of waterfowl, stretches south from the Alaska Highway and west from the Canadian border.

See also *Athabascans & Northwest Staging Route.*

◆ Northwest Passage

The Northwest Passage—a water route from the Atlantic Ocean to the Pacific Ocean—was sought by explorers for almost 400 years, beginning in the 16th century. In the early 19th century, after repeated searches along the northwestern coast of North America, the Northwest Passage was proved to exist along the northern coast of Alaska and northern Canada. The route is too far north to allow for easy navigation.

The first expedition to cross the route was led by Norwegian explorer Roald Amundsen between 1903 and 1906. Although the route was initially sought after as a trading route, a commercial ship did not cross the passage until 1969, after the discovery of oil in Prudhoe Bay. The ice-breaking tanker *Manhattan* was the first commercial ship to cross the Northwest Passage.

See also *Oil.*

◆ Northwest Staging Route

The Northwest Staging Route—a chain of air bases from Edmonton, AB, through Whitehorse, YT, to Fairbanks—was built in a cooperative effort by the United States and Canada. The chain of bases was used to build up and supply Alaska defense during World War II; lend-lease aircraft were flown up this route to Ladd Field (now Fort Wainwright) in Fairbanks. The bases were also used during the construction of the Alaska Highway, which follows the same basic path as the staging route.

See also *Alaska Highway & Aviation.*

◆ Norton Sound

Norton Sound is on the western coast of Alaska in the Bering Sea, between the Seward Peninsula on the north and the Yukon-Kuskokwim

Delta on the south. Capt. James Cook discovered Norton Sound in 1778 and named it in honor of Sir Fletcher Norton, the speaker of the British House of Commons at the time. The sound is 125 miles long and 70 miles wide.

◆ Nulato Massacre

Nulato (pop. 359) was founded in 1838 by a Russian trader named Malakhov when he built a trading post and a few buildings on the bank of the Yukon River. While Malakhov was away from the post for a few months, Natives burned it down. The next year, after rebuilding, the incident was repeated. In 1841, the Russian-American Co. sent a man named Vasili Derzhavin to set up a new post. In one of the most chronicled events in Alaskan history, the Koyukon Indians attacked the post in 1851, killing 53 inhabitants. Among the victims were Derzhavin and Lt. John J. Barnard, a British naval officer from the HMS *Enterprise.*

Various reasons have been given for the massacre, including a trade dispute between the Europeans and Natives, the long-standing rivalry between the Lower Koyukon and Upper Koyukon Indians, or a possible insult by Lt. Barnard of the Koyukon shaman. A new fort with a stockade was built a few years later at the village's present site, a couple of miles upriver from Old Nulato.

◆ Nunivak Island

Nunivak Island, the second-largest island in the Bering Sea, is surrounded by shoals, making navigation difficult. As a result, explorers and traders were late in visiting the island. Nunivak Eskimos were able to retain ancient traditions much longer than many mainland Natives. They continued to wear labrets (lip ornaments) until the 1920s.

Nunivak is part of the nation's largest wildlife refuge, the 1.1-million-acre Yukon Delta National Wildlife Refuge. Reindeer were introduced to the island during the 1800s, and in 1935, musk oxen were imported from Greenland. Both species thrived in the predator-free habitat. No other large land animals live on the island. Native animals include foxes, weasels, lemmings, voles, shrews and mink. Today, reindeer are a major source of food and income for Nunivak residents, and musk oxen provide further means of industry.

See also *Eskimos, Ivory, Musk Oxen, Qiviut & Reindeer.*

◆ Oil

During the 19th century, Eskimos used pieces of oily tundra as fuel in their homes. Oil exploration began in Cook Inlet in 1898. The first commercial oil discovery was in 1902 at Katalla, east of Cordova; the field produced a moderate amount of oil and gas for local use until 1933.

In the early 1920s, oil was discovered seeping out of the ground at Cape Simpson, just west of Point Barrow on the Beaufort Sea. A 23-million-acre area surrounding the site was earmarked for use by the Navy as Naval Petroleum Reserve Number Four (NPR-4), or Pet-Four, but it was not developed until World War II. Drilling at NPR-4 uncovered nine oil and gas fields, but no significant finds.

The first successful commercial oil well was the Swanson River oil field on the Kenai Peninsula, brought in by Richfield Oil Company in 1957. The first petroleum refinery in Alaska was opened at nearby Nikiski in 1963 by Standard Oil.

Meanwhile, the Department of the Interior had begun leasing rights to drill on the North Slope, the region north of the Brooks Range. In 1968,

Atlantic Richfield discovered oil in Prudhoe Bay, in what was found to be the largest oil field in North America, representing 25 percent of known oil deposits in the United States. Worldwide attention focused on Alaska, and the state suddenly became a leader in the nation's oil and gas industry. The discovery led to the building of the trans-Alaska pipeline, completed in 1977 after a flurry of red tape involving land rights and environmental concerns.

The Prudhoe Bay oil fields supply Alaska with thousands of jobs and billions of dollars for capital-improvement programs and the establishment of a state savings account (the Alaska Permanent Fund). Other oil fields have been discovered on the Kenai Peninsula and in Cook Inlet, and millions of dollars are being spent on exploration in areas such as Norton Sound, on Alaska's west coast, and in the Beaufort Sea.

See also *Alaska Permanent Fund, Arctic National Wildlife Refuge, Industry, Katalla, North Slope, Prudhoe Bay & Trans-Alaska Pipeline.*

◆ Onion Portage

See *Kobuk Valley National Park.*

◆ Oogruk

The Eskimo name for the Pacific bearded seal is *oogruk*. Oogruk are found throughout the Bering and Chukchi seas, and hunters consider them a highly prized catch, making full use of the large animal's meat, oil and hide. Oogruk are a staple for subsistence hunters in the Far North.

See also *Seals.*

◆ Oosik

An oosik is the penis bone of a walrus. It is polished and sold to tourists as a curio.

See also *Walrus.*

◆ Otters

Two kinds of otters live in Alaska—river and sea. The river otter is found throughout the state, predominantly in Southeast, Prince William Sound and the Yukon-Kuskokwim Delta. The sea otter inhabits the southern coast, from Southeast west to the Aleutian Islands. The river otter is much smaller than the sea otter, weighing 10 to 25 pounds in contrast to the sea otter's

40 to 80 pounds. Another key difference is the river otter can have as many as six pups in a litter, while the sea otter has only one.

In terms of survival, the disparity between river and sea otters comes down to one element—fur. The river otter's thick brown fur is durable but has never been a widely desired commodity. However, when Vitus Bering's crew took samples of sea otter furs back to Russia in 1742, its pelt was considered the finest known to man. The furs brought incredible prices, which prompted increased hunting. During the following hundred years the sea otter population was decimated.

Russian fur companies realized overhunting would soon destroy their business, and in the early 1800s began setting limits. But after the U.S. purchase of Alaska, unlimited hunting of sea otters was again allowed and the animal had nearly become extinct by the turn of the century. In 1911, otters were given complete protection by the U.S. government, and the population has recovered during the last 80 years.

◆ Outside

To Alaskans, "Outside" is where all other Americans live, also referred to as the Lower 48.

Pack Creek Bear Observatory

Pack Creek Bear Observatory, located on the east coast of Admiralty Island within Admiralty Island National Monument, is a well-known bear-viewing spot. Access is by charter plane or by boat from Sitka or Juneau. Regulations are in effect restricting when and where visitors may go, as well as what visitors may take with them. Camping is not allowed in the area. Visitors must obtain a permit from the U.S. Forest Service or Alaska Dept. of Fish and Game office in Juneau before departing for Pack Creek.

During summer and fall, brown bears fish for spawning pink, chum and silver salmon in Pack Creek. Best time for viewing and photographing the bears is mid-July to Late August.

Pack Creek flows east into Seymour Canal, a 40-mile-long canal popular with kayakers and known for its numerous humpback whales.

See also *Admiralty Island, Anan Bear Observatory & Bears.*

Palmer

Palmer (pop. 2,866), in the Matanuska Valley, is the only community in Alaska that developed from an agricultural economy. It was the site of a unique federal relief program during the Great Depression. Under President Franklin Delano Roosevelt, 203 families were relocated from the

Midwest to the Matanuska Valley to set up farms. Palmer, which was established as a station on the Matanuska Branch of the Alaska Railroad around 1916, became the unofficial capital of the valley.

The University of Alaska operates an agricultural and forestry experiment station, a cooperative extension service office and a research farm in Palmer. Reindeer and musk oxen are also raised in the vicinity.

See also *Agriculture, Matanuska Valley Colony, Musk Oxen & Reindeer*.

◆ Panhandle

The "Panhandle" is a nickname for Southeast, which branches southward about 600 miles from Icy Bay, near Malaspina Glacier in the St. Elias Range, to the Dixon Entrance, just north of the Queen Charlotte Islands near Prince Rupert, BC.

See also *Dixon Entrance & Inside Passage*.

◆ Parka

A traditional parka is a one-piece, hooded pullover coat made of caribou hide and wolf and wolverine furs. Parkas are primarily an Eskimo article, though other Natives use them to a limited extent. In recent years, a parka has come to mean any insulated coat or jacket with a hood.

See also *Squirrels*.

◆ Pemmican

Pemmican is a Native snack consisting of dried or pounded meat, usually buffalo or venison, mixed with dried berries and animal fat.

◆ Permafrost

Permafrost evolved as a contraction of the words "permanent frost," referring to ground that stays frozen for two years or longer. The northern third of Alaska is covered with permafrost, with some patches occurring in the Interior. Permafrost forms a seal that prevents the ground from draining during warmer months, causing boggy terrain known as muskeg. The frozen ground also makes building difficult; it buckles when heated, resulting in sinking houses and warped roads.

See also *Muskeg & Trans-Alaska Pipeline*.

◆ Permanent Fund

See *Alaska Permanent Fund.*

◆ Petersburg

Petersburg is unique in that it is one of Alaska's few towns that didn't develop as a Native or Russian settlement, nor during a gold rush, railroad or pipeline boom. Petersburg (pop. 3,207) is named for a Norwegian American, Peter Buschmann, who started a salmon cannery and sawmill in 1897. The site was cleared from a thickly timbered shore and grew around the fishing and logging industries, attracting mostly Scandinavians.

Today, Petersburg is sometimes referred to as "Little Norway." It has the largest home-based halibut fleet in the state and is renowned for its shrimp, too. LeConte Glacier, the southernmost tidewater glacier on the continent, is accessible by plane or boat from Petersburg.

"In July of 1995, 295,510 persons or 48% of Alaska's population were female ... Males totaled 320,390, thus yielding a state male-female sex ratio of 108 men to every 100 females. This differs significantly from the U.S. sex ratio of only 95 men to 100 females."

— Alaska Dept. of Labor

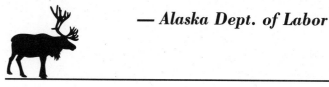

◆ Collared Pikas

These tiny members of the rabbit family weigh just 4 to 8 ounces. Most common in the Alaska Range and the southern Brooks Range, the pika has a gray or sandy coat with a lighter underside. Pikas eat all edible plant species and store dried plant matter to consume during the winter. Pikas are constantly on the move, gathering food and avoiding birds of prey. They normally live in colonies and prefer rocky, sloped terrain. Their skin is not sturdy enough to make their fur desirable.

◆ Pingos

Pingos are mounds of soil and ice that are pushed as high as 15 feet above the tundra by the pressure from water freezing and expanding underneath the soil.

◆ Pioneers' Homes

Pioneers' Homes are located in Sitka, Fairbanks, Palmer, Anchorage, Ketchikan and Juneau. These state-supported homes offer housing and care for elderly Alaskans. The homes were built to care for those people who spent most or all of their lives in Alaska, helping to build the state. To be eligible for a Pioneers' Home, a person must be at least 65 years old and have lived continuously in Alaska for 15 years or longer.

In 1913, the first Alaska Pioneers' Home was established in Sitka by the Territorial Legislature. The original buildings were two old wooden Marine barracks. In 1934, the current Sitka Pioneers' Home complex was built, which was added to the National Register of Historic Places in October 1979. The newest home, in Juneau, was built in 1988.

See also *Sourdough*.

◆ Pipeline

See *Trans-Alaska Pipeline*.

◆ Point Barrow

Point Barrow is the northernmost point in Alaska. The city of Barrow is nine miles south of the tip of the point. Capt. F.W. Beechey named the point in 1826 after Sir John Barrow, a British patron of Arctic exploration. Point Barrow's Eskimo name is *Nuwuk*, "the point."

See also *Barrow*.

◆ Point Hope

The Point Hope Peninsula is one of the oldest continuously occupied areas in North America. Bowhead whales are hunted relatively easily from the point, which juts into the Chukchi Sea in northwest Alaska. Two significant archeological sites have been excavated at Point Hope: the prehistoric Old Tigara Village, and the Ipiutak site, which consists of about 800 sod houses occupied from 500 B.C. to 100 A.D.

Capt. F.W. Beechey named the point after Sir William Johnstone Hope in 1826. During the mid-1800s, it became a commercial whaling site, until the demise of the industry in the early 1900s. The village was relocated in the 1970s, because of erosion and the threat of flooding. Every spring, the men of Point Hope continue to hunt whales from traditional skin boats, called umiaks. Visitors to the area can enjoy rockhounding, beachcombing, and bird, wildlife and whale watching.

See also *Eskimos, Whaling & Umiak.*

◆ Population

Although popular belief holds that Alaska has many more men than women, current population figures prove this to be a slight exaggeration. About 47.3 percent of Alaskans are female, compared with a national average of 51.2 percent. In other words, there are about 111 men for every 100 women in Alaska, while the rest of the United States has about 95 men for every 100 women. Some communities in Alaska do have a far less balanced ratio, such as those with economies based on the male-dominated industries of logging, mining, fishing and the military.

In Alaska, seven out of 10 people live in urban areas of 2,500 people or more. Anchorage, with 226,338 people, is the largest city in the state and 69th largest in the United States. The median age of Alaskans is younger than the national average, 28.5 for Alaskan males and 28.4 for females, compared with a national average of 31.5 and 33.8, respectively. About 10.5 percent of the state's population is military-related.

Natives account for about 15 percent of the population; this breaks down to 44,401 (8.1 percent) Eskimos, 31,245 (5.7 percent) Indians (Athabascan, Tlingit, Haida and Tsimshian) and 10,052 (1.8 percent) Aleuts. Many Natives live in rural areas with fewer than 1,000 people, although about 44 percent live in urban areas. Comparatively, 72.4 percent of the white population lives in urban areas.

◆ Porcupines

Porcupines are found throughout most of Alaska, except for the North Slope, the Seward Peninsula and the Yukon-Kuskokwim Delta. Alaska porcupines have a unique yellowish tint to their quills and hair. They are solitary animals and good swimmers; their quills are hollow and buoy them up in water. Porcupines are not hunted or trapped extensively, but they are a source of food for rural Alaskans, who can easily catch the slow-moving animals.

◆ Porpoises

See *Dolphins and Porpoises.*

◆ Portage Glacier

Portage Glacier, in Chugach National Forest, is the most-visited site in Alaska. Almost half of all the state's visitors head to Portage Valley, about 50 miles southeast of Anchorage, accessible from the Seward Highway. The Begich, Boggs Visitor Center on Portage Lake offers excellent interpretive displays on glaciation, and Forest Service interpreters are available to explain the natural and cultural history of Southcentral Alaska. A popular boat tour runs through the iceberg-filled lake to the face of the glacier. Two campgrounds are available for overnight visitors, and nature trails to Portage and Byron glaciers allow for a close-up look. Visitors are also drawn to see wildlife, such as bears, moose, otters and mountain goats, and to view iceworms on walking tours of the glacier.

Portage Glacier ended its forward advance in 1893. Since 1914, its rate of advance (about 15 feet per year) has been offset by melting at the face of the glacier. Had Portage continued to advance, it might have carved a fjord to Cook Inlet, making the Kenai Peninsula into an island. Its retreat has created a 3-mile-long, 800-foot-deep lake. The visitor center, which used to be near the face of the glacier, is now at the other end of Portage Lake from it.

Portage Glacier earned its name from its location, which allowed Tanaina Indians, Chugach Eskimos and Russian fur traders to use it as a "portage" between Cook Inlet and Prince William Sound prior to the 20th century. The Portage Valley has erratic weather conditions, including occasional hurricane-force winds; other dangers include winter avalanches and summer landslides.

For further information, contact the Chugach National Forest (address and phone in For More Information section).

See also ***Chugach National Forest.***

◆ Potlatch

The traditional potlatch was a ceremonial feast celebrated by many tribes of the Pacific Northwest coast and Natives of southeastern and western Alaska. These elaborate feasts were held to mark totem pole dedications, accessions, accomplishments such as the first killing of game by a child, the return or rescue of a relative, weddings and deaths.

In addition to feasting, singing, dancing and dramatizations, an essential part of these celebrations was the bestowing of highly valued gifts. The potlatch host would demonstrate his affluence by giving baskets, blankets, jewelry, gift boxes, even totem poles and canoes to his guests. If the host aspired to leadership within his group, he would give away all he owned and accept no aid from others for a year following the celebration.

However, a careful log was kept of all gifts given, and tribal etiquette demanded that recipients return these acts of generosity at potlatches of their own. If a gift-giver died before being repaid, the return gift was owed to his heirs. Potlatches between rival groups sometimes became highly competitive, and hosts would destroy valued items as a demonstration of their wealth.

Today, the term potlatch is used for many Native gatherings. Potlatches can last several days and the emphasis has shifted from gift-giving to feasting and celebrating.

See also *Natives.*

◆ Precipitation

See *Climate.*

◆ Pribilof Islands

In 1786, a Russian named Gavriil Pribilof spied migrating seals while sailing in the Aleutian chain. The location of the breeding grounds of the northern fur seal had long been a mystery, so Pribilof decided to follow them. Heading northward, he landed on June 12 on a remote and uninhabited island, which he named after his ship, the *St. George.* St. George Island was found to be part of a small archipelago, consisting of two larger islands and three small ones: Otter, Walrus and Sealion rocks. St. Paul, the second of the larger islands located 40 miles away from St. George, was not sighted for a year because the area is so often covered in fog.

It is now known that the Pribilof Islands have North America's largest northern fur seal and seabird colonies; they are sometimes called the Seal Islands. Archeological evidence suggests that they were not inhabited until Russian occupation in the 18th century. (The Pribilof Islands are difficult to navigate and none of the islands has a decent harbor for boats to land in.) The Russians relocated Aleuts from Unalaska and Atka to work as seal hunters, settling them in the two islands' communities of St. Paul and St. George.

After the United States purchased Alaska from Russia, it contracted with private companies to harvest the fur seals. In 1910, the federal government began managing the sealing operations. By this time, the Pribilofs' population of 3 million seals had been reduced to 300,000; the sealing industry declined as limits were enacted in an effort to repopulate the rookeries.

During World War II, Pribilof residents were evacuated to Funter Bay in Southeast Alaska.

The Pribilofs lie at the southern limit of sea ice in the Bering Sea. The economy today is based on sealing, fishing (mostly of halibut) and tourism. St. George (pop. 138) has one of the largest seabird colonies in the northern hemisphere (about 2.5 million birds nest on its cliffs each summer) and an estimated 250,000 northern fur seals congregate in its six rookeries. On St. Paul (pop. 763), more than a million seals gather each year, 211 species of birds nest on its cliffs and about 500 reindeer are raised by island residents.

See also *Aleuts, Birds & Seals.*

◆ Prince of Wales Island

Prince of Wales Island is the second-largest island in Alaska and the third largest in the United States (after Hawaii and Kodiak Island). Located in Southeast in the Alexander Archipelago, it measures 132 miles long by 45 miles wide. Communities on the island include Craig, Klawock, Thorne Bay and Hydaburg. Industry there has ranged from timber to mining and salmon fishing. Klawock was the site of the first cannery in Alaska, built in 1878. Today, logging is prevalent.

The island offers excellent backcountry recreation, such as salmon and trout fishing, canoeing and wildlife viewing. Most of the island is national forest land. It was named for the Prince of Wales of England, with the name first appearing in an 1835 treaty between Russia and Great Britain.

See also *Canneries, Craig, Islands & Timber.*

✦ Prince William Sound

In southcentral Alaska, 70-mile-wide Prince William Sound lies at the northern end of the Gulf of Alaska. The sound is famous for its natural beauty, as well as its wealth of wildlife, which includes Dall sheep, mountain goats, sea lions, sea otters, whales, harbor seals, bald eagles and salmon. A major attraction for visitors to Prince William Sound is Columbia Glacier, one of the largest tidewater glaciers on the Alaska coast.

National attention was focused on Prince William Sound in March 1989, when the oil tanker *Exxon Valdez* ran aground, causing an 11-million-gallon oil spill.

Prince William Sound was named in May 1778 by Capt. James Cook. The Prince William Sound communities of Whittier, Valdez and Cordova are connected by state ferry service.

See also *Columbia Glacier, Cordova, Valdez & Whittier.*

✦ Promyshlenniki

After Vitus Bering's crew returned to Russia in 1742 from their expedition to Alaska (from which Bering never returned), many Russian fur hunters followed the explorer's route to the New World, tempted by the high profits of the fur trade. These men, called *promyshlenniki*, faced the rough northern seas in makeshift boats, risking hunger, scurvy and hostile encounters with the Natives. By 1788, as many as 500 promyshlenniki were working for trading companies in Russian America. Their efforts to hunt increasingly scarce furbearing animals resulted in the inadvertent exploring and charting of the islands and coast of Alaska.

See also *Vitus Bering, Fur Trapping & Gregorii Shelikof.*

✦ Prudhoe Bay

The largest oil field in Alaska is located in Prudhoe Bay on the Beaufort Sea coast. The bay is 9.6 miles across and was named by a British explorer, Sir John Franklin, on Aug. 16, 1826.

See also *Industry, Oil & Trans-Alaska Pipeline.*

✦ Puffins

The puffin, a northern sea bird, is one of the most unique-looking birds in Alaska. Puffins have a large, triangular orange and yellow bill, and distinct black and white plumage. Two types of puffins can be found in the state: the tufted and the horned. The horned puffin has a white belly that distinguishes it from the tufted puffin, which sports long yellowish tufts of feathers on the back of its head. Puffins are commonly seen in the Kodiak Archipelago and the Pribilof Islands.

See also *Birds.*

"There is one word of advice and caution to be given those intending to visit Alaska for pleasure, or for sightseeing. If you are old, go by all means, but if you are young, wait. The scenery of Alaska is much grander than anything else of its kind in the world, and it is not well to dull ones' capacity for enjoyment by seeing the finest first."

— Henry Gannett, Harriman Alaska Expedition, 1899

◆ Qiviut

Qiviut is the Eskimo word for the soft underhair of the musk ox (oom-ingmak or umingmak). Qiviut supports a successful cottage industry in Alaska. The fiber—highly valued for its light weight, softness and warmth—is knitted into hats and scarves in a variety of traditional patterns by Native Alaskan knitters, and sold through a co-operative in Anchorage. Qiviut is finer than cashmere and does not shrink when washed in warm water. Although expensive, qiviut is in demand, and it has provided a stable income for a number of Native women pursuing subsistence lifestyles in remote villages in western Alaska. The wool is gathered when musk oxen shed; often it drags behind the animals, catching on bushes and the ground. One musk ox produces as much as seven pounds of qivi-ut each year.

See also *Musk Oxen*

William A. Wallace Collection

R

◆ Rafting

See *Boating, Canoeing, Kayaking and Rafting, & Rivers*.

◆ Railroads

Alaska has two operating railroads: the Alaska Railroad and the White Pass & Yukon Route. The Alaska Railroad provides service between Anchorage and Fairbanks via Denali National Park; between Portage and Whittier; and between Anchorage and Seward.

The White Pass & Yukon Route (WP&YR), a narrow-gauge railroad that originally traveled between Skagway and Whitehorse, YT, now runs from Skagway to Fraser, BC, where passengers may continue to Whitehorse by bus. The White Pass route includes only 20 miles of rail travel within Alaska. The track climbs 2,865 feet from sea level to White Pass Summit at the U.S.-Canada border.

Canadian contractor Michael J. Heney began building the rail in 1898 to transport prospectors during the Klondike gold rush. By the time it was completed in 1900, many miners had left for the gold fields at Nome. At the time, the White Pass & Yukon Route was the most northern railroad in North America. It helped the town of Skagway survive as a transportation hub after the gold stampeders moved on.

Another railway, the Copper River & Northwestern Railway (CRNW), was built in 1906, and operated between Cordova, on the gulf coast, and the copper mines at Kennicott. The CRNW (also known as the "Can't Run and Never Will") was also built by Michael Heney. It ceased operation in 1938 when the Kennecott Mine closed.

For further information on riding the rails, contact the Alaska Railroad Corp. and the White Pass & Yukon Route (addresses and phone numbers in For More Information section).

See also *Alaska Railroad, Cordova, Copper River Highway, Kennecott Copper Mine & Skagway.*

✦ RATNET

RATNET stands for the Rural Alaska Television Network, a state-operated system that broadcasts television in the Bush.

✦ Red Devil

Red Devil (pop. 53), a town on the Kuskokwim River, was named after the Red Devil Mine, which produced 2.7 million pounds of mercury—Alaska's total output—before it closed. The mine was established in 1933, after a number of quick-silver deposits were discovered in the area. It operated under various names until 1971. Cinnabar and antimony reserves were also mined. Today, access to the mine is closed because of chemical hazards.

See also *Mining.*

✦ Red Dog Mine

See *Mining.*

✦ Regions

Alaska is traditionally divided into six geographic regions. The Arctic region lies above the Arctic Circle, bordered by the Brooks Range on the south and the Arctic Sea coast on the north. Interior Alaska is the central area between the Brooks Range and the Alaska Range, with Fairbanks as its hub of commercial activity.

The southcentral region curves along the southern part of Alaska from the Gulf of Alaska coast to the Alaska Range, and includes the state's most populous city, Anchorage, and the fertile Matanuska and Susitna river valleys.

Southeast Alaska is the forested "panhandle" extending about 600 miles southward from Icy Bay on the Gulf of Alaska coast to the Dixon Entrance south of Ketchikan. Southeast includes the hundreds of islands that make up the Alexander Archipelago.

Western Alaska, or the Bering Sea coast, reaches from Bristol Bay north to the Seward Peninsula, and includes the Yukon-Kuskokwim Delta.

In the southwest region, the Alaska Peninsula and Aleutian Islands extend more than 1,600 miles from Mt. Iliamna into the Pacific Ocean, encompassing the Kodiak Island group.

See also *Alaska Peninsula, Alaska Range, Aleutian Islands, Alexander Archipelago, Arctic Circle, Bristol Bay, Brooks Range, Climate, Gulf of Alaska, Inside Passage & Yukon-Kuskokwim Delta.*

◆ Reindeer

Reindeer, a type of domesticated caribou, were originally imported from Siberia during the late 19th century to supplement Alaska Natives' food sources. The missionary Sheldon Jackson was instrumental in importing reindeer to Native settlements. Reindeer increase rapidly when they have no predators, and thus have been successfully raised in places such as Nunivak Island in the Bering Sea.

Reindeer contribute to the economy in western Alaska, in communities on the Seward and Baldwin peninsulas, such as Teller, Shishmaref and Nome, and in other areas throughout the state, such as Palmer in southcentral Alaska. The antlers are clipped annually and sold to Asian markets, where they are ground and sold as aphrodisiacs. Reindeer meat is sold commercially in Alaska, and the hides are used for a variety of purposes, such as sled covers and mukluks.

See also *Sheldon Jackson & Nunivak Island.*

◆ Libby Riddles

In 1985, Libby Riddles became the first woman to win the Iditarod Trail Sled Dog Race. Since then, another woman, Susan Butcher, has won the race four times, in 1986, '87, '88 and '90.

See also *Iditarod Trail Sled Dog Race.*

◆ Rivers

Alaska has more than 3,000 rivers. The five longest are the Yukon (1,875 miles), the Koyukuk (554 miles), the Kuskokwim (540 miles), the Tanana (531 miles) and the Innoko (463 miles). The Yukon ranks third in the United States in length, after the Mississippi and Missouri rivers. Its total length in Alaska and Canada is 2,300 miles. The Porcupine, another major river, flows 550 miles, but only one-third of its length is in Alaska.

Many of Alaska's rivers are part of the National Wild and Scenic Rivers System. The system protects rivers of exceptional scenic, recreational, geologic, historic or cultural value. For further information on the 25 national wild and scenic rivers in Alaska contact the Alaska Public Lands Information Center (address and phone in For More Information section). For information on river activities, consult *The ALASKA WILDERNESS GUIDE,* available from Vernon Publications.

See also *Boating, Canoeing, Kayaking and Rafting; McNeil River; Yukon River & Yukon-Kuskokwim Delta.*

◆ Roadhouses

Roadhouses, spaced about a day's travel by horseback apart, provided food and shelter for early-day travelers in Alaska. Roadhouses sprang up in the late 19th and early 20th century, as a growing number of people traveled the rough roads and trails between settlements. Mail carriers, who traveled by dog sled, and riverboat passengers also relied on the hostelries.

Most roadhouses included a few outbuildings, a stable, a corral and sheds. They received supplies during summer and were self-sufficient during the long winter months.

Roadhouses became less necessary as the 20th century advanced. The introduction of the automobile and later the airplane led to the closure of many. Of the hundreds of original roadhouses, only a few have survived, including Gakona Roadhouse, Paxson Lodge and Talkeetna Roadhouse. Today, the word roadhouse is synonymous with lodge or hotel.

◆ Russell Lake

See *Hubbard Glacier.*

◆ Russian-American Co.

In 1799, Russia consolidated all the companies operating in America into the Russian-American Co. in order to administer the fur industry in Alaska. For the next 68 years, the Russian-American Co. was the only governing power in Alaska. At first, it had exclusive trading privileges in the area north of 55°N latitude. Then, in 1826, Russia negotiated treaties with Great Britain and the United States that extended its control down to 54°40' N.

Alexander Baranof was the company's manager until 1817. He headquartered first at Kodiak and later Sitka, with outposts as far south as

California. When Baranof was replaced, the company began to go downhill. His successors were naval officers who were less interested in the trade business. Other factors leading to the company's demise were increased competition from the British and Americans, accompanied by a simultaneous decline in the overhunted furbearing animals of Alaska, and Russia's depleted treasury following the Crimean War. Consequently, Russia became eager to sell the land, and in 1867, the United States purchased Alaska.

See also *Alaska Purchase, Alexander Baranof & Gregorii Shelikof.*

◆ Russian Orthodox Church

Around the turn of the 18th century, when the Russian-American Co. began establishing operations in Alaska, Russian Orthodox missionaries followed the fur traders to the new land to convert the Natives to Christianity. Father Herman, who was a member of the original mission sent to Kodiak from the Valaam Monastery in Russian Finland, helped build the first Russian Orthodox church at Kodiak in 1794. He was later canonized, becoming St. Herman in 1970. The Russian Orthodox faith is still practiced at churches in Karluk, Akhiok, Old Harbor and other communities on Kodiak Island. The New Valaam Monastery is located at Pleasant Harbor on Spruce Island, 12 miles north of Kodiak, near St. Herman's grave; the degree-granting St. Herman's Theological Seminary is located in Kodiak.

Through its missions, the church emphasized education. Literacy

became widespread among many Native groups, especially in the Aleutians. In 1834, the first book ever printed in an Alaska Native language—a revised Aleut catechism—was published by a missionary named Ivan Veniaminov.

Sitka became the capital of Russian Alaska in 1799, and another center of the Russian Orthodox faith when Bishop Innocent Veniaminov built St. Michael's Cathedral between 1844 and 1848. The church was destroyed by fire in January 1966. The townspeople saved many priceless icons, some brought from Russia in the early 1800s, and built a replica of the original cathedral.

Russian Orthodox churches are also found in Juneau, Ninilchik, Seldovia, Kenai, Naknek, Akutan, New Stuyahok, Newhalen, Nushagak, Pedro Bay and many other communities in southwestern and western Alaska.

See also *Russian-American Co. & Sitka.*

✦ St. Elias Range

On July 16, 1741, Capt. Cmdr. Vitus Bering sighted Mt. St. Elias, the second-highest mountain in Alaska. Bering had sailed from Siberia to the Gulf of Alaska, becoming the first European to sight the northwest coast of North America.

The St. Elias Range extends along the Alaska-Canada border, from the Panhandle into the Wrangell-St. Elias National Park, where it merges with the Wrangell Mountains. Mt. Logan, in the Canadian portion of the range, has the highest peak (19,850 feet), with Mt. St. Elias second-highest at 18,008 feet. Other major peaks in the range include Mt. Bona (16,421), Mt. Vancouver (15,300) and Mt. Hubbard (14,950). Altogether, the range has more than two dozen peaks over 10,000 feet and more than 50 glaciers with lengths of more than 5 miles (including Hubbard, Malaspina and the glaciers of Glacier Bay).

See also *Vitus Bering, Glacier Bay National Park, Hubbard Glacier, Malaspina Glacier & Wrangell-St. Elias National Park.*

✦ St. Lawrence Island

St. Lawrence Island, in the Bering Sea, has been inhabited for several thousand years. Yup'ik Eskimos, whose name for the island is *Sivuqaq,* cultivated a complex and relatively isolated culture, discovered by Capt. Cmdr. Vitus Bering on St. Lawrence Day, Aug. 10, 1728. The islanders have relied mainly on walrus and gray and bowhead whales for their livelihood.

Reindeer, which were introduced to the island in 1900, have become an important part of the economy, too.

The two main communities, Gambell (pop. 525) and Savoonga (pop. 519), continue to have subsistence-based economies, supplemented by income from the sale of ivory carvings, a traditional Eskimo art. Savoonga was established as a reindeer camp in 1969, and has grown into a sizable community. Its nickname is "The Walrus Capital of the World," and each spring a Walrus Festival is held there. In the past 50 years, St. Lawrence Islanders have also turned the sale of excavated artifacts into a means of income. In 1989, the National Register of Historic Places stripped five prehistoric village sites of their historic landmark designation because of extensive looting by villagers.

See also *Eskimos, Ivory, Reindeer & Walrus*.

◆ St. Michael

The town of St. Michael (pop. 295), on St. Michael Island in Norton Sound, was a major gateway to the Interior during the gold rush era at the turn of the century. River traffic heading to the Klondike gold fields often began its journey at St. Michael. During the Nome gold rush in 1900, the island's population skyrocketed to an estimated 10,000 people at the height of the stampede, though many left after only a few months. St. Michael remained an important transshipment point until the Alaska Railroad was built, as the village has the closest deepwater port to the Yukon and Kuskokwim rivers.

The Russians were the first non-Natives to inhabit the island. In 1833, they established a stockade, or *redoubt*, which was the northernmost Russian settlement in Alaska. An Eskimo village, Tachik, was also located on the east side of the island. After the U.S. purchase of Alaska, the U.S. built a military post, Fort St. Michael, in 1897; but it closed in 1922.

Today, the remnants of St. Michael's past can still be seen, including three Russian houses, the hulls of old steamboats and several old cemeteries. The sites of the old Russian and U.S. forts are on the National Register of Historic Places.

See also *Gold & Yukon-Kuskokwim Delta*.

◆ Salmon

Historically, the most valuable fish in the Pacific has been the salmon. Five Pacific salmon species are found in Alaska waters: sockeye, king, pink, coho and chum salmon.

Sockeye (red) salmon weigh 3 to 7 pounds and normally fetch the highest prices for commercial fishermen. Landlocked sockeye are called kokanee. King salmon (chinook) are the largest of all salmon and probably the most sought-after sportfish. The average king weighs between 15 and 30 pounds; reigning sportfish trophy king is 97 pounds 4 ounces. Pink (humpback) salmon are the smallest of the species, averaging 4 pounds, and the most abundant. Pinks are also the least commercially valuable of the 5 salmon species, although they provide a large percentage of the salmon harvest. Coho (silver) salmon average 9 pounds and are a popular sportfish. Chum (dog) salmon seldom strike lures and are a poor game fish. Most chums, which average 9 pounds, are taken by commercial fishermen and used for canning. Though flavorful, their light pink flesh becomes almost white after being canned and is considered less attractive—and less valuable—than canned red salmon. Spawning chum males develop a sharply hooked nose and doglike teeth.

Salmon are anadromous, spawning in fresh water and maturing in the sea. Salmon lay their eggs in streams, rivers and lakes; the young fry are born three to four months later. After heading out to sea, the fish return years later to the exact location of their hatching ground, a homing instinct so precise that it continues to mystify scientists. After spawning, all Pacific salmon die, their carcasses becoming food for many different animals and birds.

All species are taken in both fresh water and salt water, although restrictions apply according to region. Commercial salmon harvest is by purse seine and gill net (set and drift), with some trolling. Fish wheels account for less than one percent of the commercial salmon harvest.

Salmon can be dried, smoked, canned, salted or frozen. Salmon is historically an important food source for Alaska Natives.

◆ Sea Disasters

In the early hours of the morning on Oct. 24, 1918, the passenger vessel the S.S. *Princess Sophia*, with 350 people on board, hit Vanderbilt Reef in Lynn Canal, north of Juneau. Stormy seas and a high tide forced the boat off the reef, and on the evening of Oct. 25, the *Sophia* sank; the entire crew and all the passengers perished. A navigation light on Vanderbilt Reef now warns ships to steer clear and avoid the fate of the *Sophia*.

The frigid seas around Alaska have claimed the lives of many people throughout the years. In February 1946, the S.S. *Yukon*, bound from Seward to Seattle with 496 passengers and 124 crewmen aboard, ran aground on rocks at 4 a.m. The pilot had miscalculated the ship's location and stranded it in rough seas with a broken stern, in winds of 37 mph.

A number of vessels responded to the distress calls, including a Coast Guard cutter, a Navy tug and transport vessel, and two minesweepers. Some passengers were rescued within hours of the accident, but others had to wait aboard the ship or on the icy beach until rescue boats could reach them during the next few days. The survivors were taken to Seward, where townspeople housed them while they recovered. All told, 11 men died. The captain, C.E. Trondsen, was later charged with negligence.

An interesting and less tragic sea adventure occurred in 1908, after the S.S. *Ohio* steamed out of Seattle on June 1, headed for Nome. The captain of the ship was under orders from the owner to avoid any ice damage when they traveled through the Bering Sea, as the *Ohio* had nearly sunk the previous year after it hit an ice floe.

The Seattle-to-Nome trip normally took about 10 days, but the *Ohio* was at sea for a record 40 days. When the *Ohio* was only 35 miles from Nome, Capt. Conradi, heeding the orders of the owner, decided the sea was too treacherous for him to continue. Although many other boats passed through the ice pack to Nome, for weeks Capt. Conradi anchored the *Ohio* or let it drift southward with the ice, restocking with coal at Dutch Harbor. The passengers were near mutiny by the time two U.S. Revenue cutters ordered Conradi to follow them through the ice pack to Nome. No one on shore had heard from the boat in weeks, and many worried it was lost at sea. All 600 passengers finally stepped safely to shore after a harrowing six weeks.

See also *Whaling.*

◆ Sea Ice

Although not the land of ice and snow pictured in popular fiction, part of Alaska is surrounded by a sea of ice during several months of the year. In the Arctic Ocean, the Chukchi Sea is ice-covered for about half the year, while the Beaufort Sea may be ice-covered for as long as 10 months each year. Permanent pack ice occurs only along the far northern coast of Alaska (generally, north of 72°N latitude).

Sea water freezes at about 29°F; and as it freezes—from the shore outward to the sea—it loses its salt content, becoming freshwater ice. New ice forms each fall, reaching thicknesses of six feet. Residual sea ice may be 30 feet thick. Ocean currents and wind push sea ice, forming pressure ridges between stationary and moving ice. These ridges may protrude more than 20 feet up from the ice pack, and even farther below the surface.

See also **Breakup, Glaciers, Ice Fields, Ice Fog, Icebergs & Permafrost.**

◆ Sea Lions

Alaska is home to the Steller sea lion, a much larger relative of the California sea lion. Steller sea lion bulls can reach 13 feet in length and may weigh as much as 2,400 pounds. Females are about half that size, averaging 7 feet in length and 700 to 800 pounds in weight.

Sea lions live in coastal waters from Southeast to the tip of the Aleutians. During summer they are also found in the Pribilof Islands, although some migrate as far south as California. They prefer remote islands with clear, shallow water and abundant fish. At their summer rookeries, a male sea lion may have 15 or more females in his harem. Since the enactment of the Marine Mammal Protection Act in 1972, only Alaskan Natives may hunt sea lions.

◆ Seals

The northern fur seal is Alaska's only fur-bearing seal; it is found in coastal waters from Southeast to Bristol Bay. Their primary habitat is the Pribilof Islands, which are home to eighty

percent of the world's northern fur-seal population. During summer, about a million fur seals can be found in the Pribilof rookeries, which empty by December when the seals migrate south for the winter. Like the sea otter, the fur seal was hunted nearly to extinction during the 1800s. In 1911, the U.S. government banned hunting of the fur seal, and its numbers have increased steadily since then. A male fur seal weighs between 300 and 500 pounds; a female about 100 pounds.

Harbor seals also reside in the Pribilof Islands, and are found in the Aleutian chain and along Alaska's southern coast. A freshwater colony of harbor seals lives in Iliamna Lake. Feeding on fish and crustaceans, harbor seals are unpopular with fishermen who compete with them for salmon.

In the north, the Bering and Chukchi seas are home to the spotted, ringed, ribbon and Pacific bearded seals. The ringed seal is similar in appearance to the harbor seal, with yellowish rings or blotches. It is the most capable of the seal family at living under solid ice. It constantly maintains breathing holes in the ice. The spotted seal has a silvery coat with dark patterns. The ribbon seal has stark markings of white bands on a darker background, while the females have a less pronounced contrast. Most of the ribbon seal population live in the northern central Bering Sea, and are not easily available to hunters.

The Pacific bearded seal, however, is actively hunted and highly prized by Eskimo hunters, whose name for it is *oogruk*. Adults may weigh as much as 750 pounds in winter. Distributed widely throughout the Bering and Chukchi seas, they follow the seasonal advance and retreat of ice. Native populations hunt seals for food, and utilize their skins and intestines for a variety of purposes, from boats to raincoats.

See also *Oogruk & Pribilof Islands.*

◆ Seward

Known as "The Gateway to Kenai Fjords National Park," Seward (pop. 2,699) lies at the northwest end of Resurrection Bay on the east coast of the Kenai Peninsula. The town, at the foot of Mt. Marathon, is perhaps best known for its annual Fourth of July endurance race—the Mount Marathon Race®—and for its well-attended silver salmon derby each August.

The Seward area was explored in 1791 by Alexander Baranof, manager of the Russian-American Co. He named the bay after it sheltered him from a storm he encountered while enroute from Kodiak to Yakutat on the Russian Sunday of the Resurrection. In 1903, the town of Seward was established by railroad surveyors, and chosen to be the ocean terminal for the Alaska Railroad. The tracks were completed in 1923, connecting it to Anchorage.

Seward was named for Secretary of State William Henry Seward, who negotiated the purchase of Alaska in 1867. Today, Seward's economy is based on the tourism, fisheries, timber and cargo industries. Its harbor is ice-free year-round.

See also *Alexander Baranof & Kenai Fjords National Park.*

◆ William Henry Seward

William Henry Seward, secretary of state under President Abraham Lincoln, was an active expansionist. He successfully negotiated the purchase of Alaska from Russia, and advocated the acquisition of Greenland, Iceland, Hawaii and the Danish West Indies. Seward, who lost the 1860

Republican presidential nomination to Lincoln, was appointed secretary of state after Lincoln was elected. The one-time political rivals developed a trusting relationship.

Seward was shot when Lincoln was assassinated. John Wilkes Booth had intended to kill Seward along with Lincoln, but Seward survived. Seward continued as secretary of state under president Andrew Johnson. In 1867, he signed a treaty with Russia, purchasing Alaska for $7.2 million. The American public scoffed at the deal, calling Alaska "Seward's Icebox" and "Seward's Folly."

◆ Seward Peninsula

The 200-mile-long Seward Peninsula extends into the Bering Sea on the northwest coast of Alaska. Bounded to the north by the Chukchi Sea, to the south by Norton Sound, and to the west by Bering Strait, it was named for William Henry Seward. Nome is the largest community on the peninsula. The Diomede Islands lie off the tip of the Seward Peninsula.

◆ Seward's Day

Seward's Day, an Alaska state holiday, is celebrated on the last Monday in March. It commemorates the signing of the treaty by which the United States bought Alaska from Russia.

◆ Gregorii Shelikof

Gregorii Shelikof is credited with founding the first Russian colony in Alaska. Shelikof built a permanent settlement on Kodiak Island in 1784, largely to protect his company's commercial interests in Alaska's fur trade. He named the colony Three Saints Bay, after his ship. Shelikof hired Alexander Baranof in 1790 as manager of the Russian-American Co. The 150-mile-long water passage between the Alaska Peninsula and Kodiak Island was named Shelikof Strait by another Russian in 1831.

See also *Alexander Baranof, Vitus Bering & Russian-American Co.*

◆ Shemya Island

Shemya Island, located near the west end of the Aleutian chain, has been called "The Black Pearl of the Aleutians," because of its black, volcanic sand beaches, and "The Rock," because of its rocky and steep cliffs. It was the site of Shemya Air Force Base, which closed in 1997.

In May 1943, Shemya became involved in World War II when the Army landed 2,500 troops on the island to construct runways. Bombing missions were flown from Shemya from March 16, 1944 until Aug. 13, 1945.

Shemya has recorded the strongest winds in the state, measured at 139 mph.

See also *Aleutian Islands & World War II*.

◆ Shrews

Seven species of the high-strung shrew live in Alaska. The tiny, fast-moving animals have a long nose and dense brown or gray fur. Shrews must eat almost constantly to keep up with their high metabolisms, and are so high-strung they may die of fright from a sudden shock, such as a clap of thunder. Some shrews grow to only 3 inches in length, yet they will attack other shrews, or larger mice or birds when they are hungry. Shrews are active year-round and live in many areas around the state.

◆ Sitka

In 1799, Alexander Baranof built a trading post and fort (St. Michael's Redoubt) on what is now known as Baranof Island in the Alexander Archipelago. The Tlingit Indians burned down the fort, and in 1804 Baranof returned from Kodiak to rebuild a few miles north. By 1808, the new site was the capital of Russian Alaska. The Russians called it New Archangel, although the Tlingit name—Sitka—eventually won out.

Baranof erected a large home in Sitka that came to be known as Baranof's Castle, and the hill on which it sat is called Castle Hill. The "castle" burned down in 1894; today, only a few cannons remain. The hill was also the site of the official exchange of Alaska from Russia to the United States in 1867. Sitka remained the capital of Alaska until 1900, when the territorial government was moved to Juneau. The city receives many visitors each year who are interested in its Russian, American and Tlingit heritage.

Sitka (pop. 8,588) is the fourth-largest city in Alaska. It is protected from the ocean by myriad small islands and Cape Edgecumbe. Mt. Edgecumbe (3,201 feet), a dormant volcano, rises above the city and is often compared with the classic shape of Mt. Fuji in Japan. Sitka's economy has traditionally been based on salmon fishing, although the tourism and timber industries play an important role, and the government provides a number of jobs.

See also *Alaska Purchase, Alexander Baranof, Russian Orthodox Church, Sitka National Historical Park & Tlingit Indians*.

◆ Sitka National Historical Park

Sitka National Historical Park, a 106-acre park on Baranof Island, preserves the community's Tlingit and Russian heritage. The park marks the site of the last major resistance of the Tlingit Indians to Russian colonization. In 1804, Alexander Baranof led Russian troops to victory in the Battle of Sitka. The Tlingits were defeated after they ran out of ammunition. Along with the 1804 battle site and fort, the park includes the Russian Bishop's House (built in 1842 and one of the most significant historical structures in Alaska), and a collection of 18 Tlingit and Haida totem poles.

See also *Alexander Baranof & Sitka.*

◆ Sitka Slippers

In southeastern Alaska, big, rubber boots worn for trekking through mud during the rainy seasons are sometimes called Sitka slippers.

◆ Skagway

The town of Skagway sprang up almost overnight in July 1897, as thousands of gold-seekers arrived to follow the White Pass and Chilkoot trails to the Yukon gold fields. By October of the same year, Skagway's population was estimated to be 20,000. The first white settlers at the site, on the north end of the Alaska Panhandle in Taiya Inlet, were William Moore and his son, who arrived in 1887 and named the area Mooresville. After hordes of prospectors stampeded to Skagway, Moore's claim was ignored and surveyors laid out the new town, originally called Skaguay. Its name came from the Skagway River, whose Tlingit name is said to mean "home of the north wind."

Skagway's first years were a flurry of activity, largely devoid of law and order. But by 1900, most of the prospectors had left to try their luck in the Nome gold rush. The town survived as a port and the terminus of the White Pass & Yukon Route railway, which ran from Skagway to Lake Bennett.

Today, tourism is Skagway's main industry. The Klondike Gold Rush National Historical Park is a major attraction, with false-fronted buildings and boardwalks from the town's gold rush days. Other attractions include the Trail of '98 Museum and the Corrington Museum of Alaska History, the ghost town of Dyea and the Chilkoot Trail. Skagway (pop. 692) is easily accessible; it is the northern terminus of the Alaska Marine Highway and a gateway city to the Alaska Highway.

See also *Chilkoot Trail, Gold, Klondike Gold Rush National Historical Park, Railroads & Jefferson "Soapy" Smith.*

◆ Skiing

Southeast of Anchorage in the Chugach Mountains, Alyeska Resort is the state's largest ski area. Owned and operated by Seibu Group of Japan since 1980, Alyeska Resort has a quad chair lift, three double chair lifts and two pony tows. Ski season is generally from November through May. Other downhill ski areas near Anchorage include Alpenglow at Arctic Valley and Hilltop Ski Area.

Miles of groomed cross-country trails are maintained by the Municipality of Anchorage in local parks. Chugach State Park, Hatcher Pass Recreation Area and Turnagain Pass are also popular destinations for cross-country skiers. Many shorter cross-country trails are maintained by municipalities near Anchorage.

Near Fairbanks, downhill skiers head to Cleary Summit, Skiland and Eielson Air Force Base and Fort Wainwright ski hills. Cross-country skiing is available at Birch Hill Recreation Area and Chena Hot Springs. Trails are also maintained by the University of Alaska Fairbanks.

Near Juneau, Eaglecrest Ski Area on Douglas Island offers both downhill and cross-country skiing. Ski season is generally from late November to early April.

Each April, Valdez is the site of the World Extreme Skiing Championships. Competitors in the event are shuttled to the top of selected peaks in the Chugach Mountains; from there they make their way down 40- to 60-degree slopes to the bottom.

For information on the variety of ski opportunities in Alaska, contact the Alaska Division of Tourism (address and phone in For More Information section).

◆ Skin Sewing

The art of skin sewing is a time-tested skill for the Eskimos and Athabascan Indians of Alaska. Skin clothing, including boots, or mukluks, and parkas, is essential to survival in the northern climate. Although many Natives have been quick to adopt modern western clothing, during wintertime traditional clothing continues to perform the best.

Eskimos fashion clothing with waterproof seams out of seal, reindeer, caribou and polar bear skins. The Athabascans use hides from caribou, moose and smaller animals, with wolf or wolverine furs for ruff. The styles, materials and decorations vary depending on the region and time of year. Animal sinew was commonly used for thread, and is still a preferred material, although dental floss will suffice if sinew is unavailable. Aside from parkas and footgear, skin sewers also manufacture cases for tools, gloves, mittens, dolls and masks.

See also *Beadwork*.

◆ Skookum

Skookum, a word meaning strong, serviceable or smart, developed from the Chinook trade jargon, which combined words from the many different languages of traders and Natives throughout Alaska and the Pacific Northwest.

◆ Sled Dogs

Sled dogs may be any breed or cross-breed. The three most common breeds are the AKC-recognized Siberian husky, Alaskan malamute and Samoyed. The Siberian husky often has blue eyes, but they may also be brown or parti-colored (one brown, one blue). The malamute is much larger than the Siberian husky and recognized more for its hauling skills than its speed. The Samoyed, one of the oldest known dog breeds, is pure white. The "Alaskan husky" is a catch-all term for any of the arctic breeds or northern types of dogs, and may be a cross-breed. Other strains common in racing dogs include Labrador, wolf and Irish setter. Mushers consider physique and mental attitude, not pedigree, when choosing a dog for competition.

Two of Alaska's most famous sled dogs were Leonhard Seppala's Togo and Balto. Togo, a purebred Siberian husky, and Balto, a freight sledding dog, played key roles in the 1925 serum run to Nome. Togo, considered to be the greatest lead dog in Alaska, took the longest leg of the relay and endured gale force winds. But it was Balto who received the acclaim by leading the final relay into Nome during a fierce white-out.

See also *Dog Mushing & Iditarod Trail Sled Dog Race.*

◆ Sleeping Lady

The "Sleeping Lady" is a local name for Mt. Susitna, located west of Anchorage. Its silhouette resembles a reclining woman.

◆ Jefferson Randolph "Soapy" Smith

During the Days of '98, as thousands of gold-seekers poured into Skagway, one man, a confident and suave Georgian in his mid-thirties, became known as the boss of the town. His name was Jefferson "Soapy" Smith.

Smith had acquired his name from an earlier scam in Leadville, Colorado, in which he deceived people into buying cakes of soap for $5, leading them to believe a twenty dollar bill would be hidden under the wrapper. Soapy Smith was an acknowledged master of the con game and he reached the pinnacle of his success while in Skagway. Using coercion, bribes, bullying and plain intimidation, Smith established a syndicate of con artists, pimps and cutthroats. At the height of power, he controlled the town's newspapers, businessmen, law enforcement and merchants.

Finally, in July 1898, the residents of Skagway turned against Soapy Smith, and he was killed in a shootout. His empire soon dissolved, and Skagway developed into a more respectable frontier community.

See also *Skagway*.

◆ Snow Machining

In wintertime, snow machines (or snowmobiles) are essential to residents of Alaska's bush villages—for transportation, hauling and recreation. Trappers and homesteaders alike rely on the machines to traverse the snowy landscape. Many urban Alaskans favor snow machines over skis or snowshoes for recreational backcountry travel. (Wilderness trails are strictly divided between motorized and non-motorized usage.) But devotees of dog mushing believe the convenience of simply starting up a machine over feeding and caring for a dog team is outweighed by the possibility of a snow machine breaking down or running out of gas in the wilderness. One of the biggest dangers of snow machining is that rider and machine may be too heavy for the ice and break through; every year more than one snowmobiler is lost this way.

◆ Soldotna

Soldotna (pop. 3,482) was established in the 1940s because of its strategic location at the junction of the Sterling and Kenai Spur highways. The town is a sportfishing and business center for the Kenai Peninsula. Its economy also draws from the oil industry in Cook Inlet. Soldotna's name comes from that of a nearby stream, which was derived from the Russian word for soldier, *soldat*. The town's museum—the Soldotna Historical Society Museum—features wildlife displays and a historic log village.

◆ Sourdough

A sourdough is an oldtimer, the opposite of a greenhorn or cheechako. The name comes from sourdough bread, a staple of early Alaska homesteaders. Originally the term meant an early settler or prospector who probably used the hardy mixture; but today, a sourdough may be anyone who has lived in Alaska for most or all of his or her life.

See also *Cheechako*.

◆ Squaw Candy

Squaw candy is a name for dried strips of salmon, a traditional Native snack.

◆ Squirrels

The squirrel family has four representatives in Alaska: the hoary marmot, the arctic ground squirrel, the red squirrel and the northern flying squirrel. The hoary marmot, an oversize squirrel weighing up to 20 pounds, is found throughout the mountainous regions of Alaska at mid to high elevations. The marmot may hibernate nine months a year. They are an important food source for Eskimos, and their skins—valued for durability and beauty—are used mainly for making parkas.

The arctic ground squirrel, however, has earned the nickname "parka squirrel." Its warm, inexpensive fur is not very durable but is sometimes used for making parkas. Arctic ground squirrels weigh only 2 pounds on average, and live in well-drained tundra areas throughout the state.

The red squirrel is smaller than the arctic, weighing about 8 ounces. Red squirrels are found almost anywhere spruce trees grow, as spruce seeds are their main food source. A chattery, and predominantly solitary animal, the red squirrel remains active all winter.

The smallest and least commonly seen squirrel in Alaska is the northern flying squirrel. Weighing 3 to 5 ounces, flying squirrels have a fur-covered membrane between their front and rear legs that allows them to leap from high places and glide long distances. Found throughout the interior, southcentral and southeast areas of Alaska, the northern flying squirrel is nocturnal and rarely sighted in the wild.

◆ State Fairs

Alaska has a variety of state fairs, which are held during the months of August and September: the Tanana Valley State Fair in Fairbanks, the

Southeast Alaska State Fair in Haines, the Alaska State Fair in Palmer and the Kodiak State Fair and Rodeo in Kodiak. For further information contact the Alaska Division of Tourism (address and phone in For More Information section).

◆ State Parks

Alaska has the largest state park system in the nation. With more than 3 million acres, Alaska makes up almost one-third of America's total state park acreage. The state park system contains 127 units designated according to use as state parks, recreation sites, recreation areas, historical parks, state trails, wilderness parks or marine parks. These are managed according to their location by 6 area offices: Kenai Peninsula, Southeast, Northern, Kodiak, Chugach/Southwest, Matanuska-Susitna and Copper River Basin. Wood-Tikchik State Park, 300 air-miles west of Anchorage, is the largest state park in the U.S., with 1.5 million acres of wilderness. The Chilkat Bald Eagle Preserve attracts the largest congregation of bald eagles in North America each fall.

Public-use cabins are available for rent in several parks on a reservation basis. For more detailed information consult *The ALASKA WILDERNESS GUIDE* and *The MILEPOST®*, both available from Vernon Publications Inc., or contact Alaska State Parks (address and phone in For More Information section).

See also *Cabins, Camping and Hiking.*

◆ State Symbols

Bird: The willow ptarmigan, adopted in 1955, is a small arctic grouse, common in much of Alaska. It lives among willows and on the open tundra.

Fish: King salmon, adopted 1962.

Flag: In 1926, Alaska held a flag design contest, which was won by a seventh-grade student named Benny Benson. Benson was award-

William A. Wallace Collection

ed a $1,000 scholarship and a watch for his design of eight gold stars (representing the Big Dipper and the North Star) on a navy blue background.

Flower: The wild forget-me-not, adopted in 1917, sports clumps of yellow-centered blue flowers. Though frail in appearance, the perennial is hardy enough to withstand the northern climate and grows throughout Alaska. The forget-me-not's leaves are grayish-green, and it grows to about 18 inches high.

Fossil: Woolly mammoth, adopted 1986. (Of the several woolly mammoths recovered from the permafrost in Alaska, perhaps the best known is a steppe bison recovered near Fairbanks. Nicknamed "Blue Babe", the bison is on display at the University of Alaska Museum in Fairbanks.)

Gem: Jade, adopted as the state gem in 1968, mostly occurs north of the Arctic Circle in Alaska, near the Dall and Kobuk rivers. The stones may be green, brown, black, yellow, white or red, the most valuable coloring being a marbled green, black or white. Jade mining increased in the second half of the 20th century after the invention of the portable wire saw, used for cutting large boulders into easily transportable pieces. Jade is used in jewelry-making and a variety of ornamental purposes, such as in clocks and furniture.

Marine Mammal: Bowhead whale, adopted 1983.

Mineral: Gold, adopted 1968.

Motto: "North to the Future," chosen in 1967 during the Alaska Purchase Centennial, was created by Juneau newsman Richard Peter. The motto is meant to represent Alaska as a land of promise.

Alaska State Library, Dobbs PCA 12-214

Seal: The Alaska State Seal depicts Native people, fur seal rookeries, the northern lights and icebergs, and the industries of mining, fisheries, railroads and agriculture. The seal was first designed in 1884 and was revised in 1910 by the Territorial Legislature. When Alaska became a state, it adopted the seal in its constitution.

Sport: Dog Mushing, adopted 1972.

Tree: The Sitka spruce, adopted in 1962, is found in coastal forests from the Kenai Peninsula to northern California. The trees may live as long as 750 years; they normally grow between 100 and 160 feet high, but may reach 225 feet. One of the most dominant tree species in Southeast, the Sitka spruce is the only conifer on Kodiak and Afognak islands.

Song: "Alaska's Flag," a poem written by Marie Drake (1888-1963), the assistant commissioner of education, which appeared on the cover of the department's bulletin in October 1935. Set to music composed by Elinor Dusenbury, and adopted as the territorial song in 1955.

> *Eight stars of gold on a field of blue—Alaska's flag.*
> *May it mean to you the blue of the sea, the evening sky.*
> *The mountain lakes, and the flowers nearby;*
> *The gold of the early sourdough's dreams,*
> *The precious gold of the hills and streams;*
> *The brilliant stars in the Northern sky,*
> *The "Bear"—the "Dipper"—and, shining high,*
> *The great North Star with its steady light,*
> *Over land and sea a beacon bright.*
> *Alaska's flag—to Alaskans dear,*
> *The simple flag of a last frontier.*

◆ Statehood

The fight for Alaska statehood began in the early 20th century, after gold rushes in the North brought national attention to Alaska. Since the Alaska purchase in 1867, Alaska had been under the jurisdiction of the U.S. Army (1867-1877), the U.S. Treasury Department (1877-1879) and the U.S. Navy (1879-1884), before becoming the District of Alaska in 1884 with a territorial governor appointed by the president.

In 1906, Alaska was given a non-voting delegate in Washington. In 1912, Congress passed a bill written by Judge James Wickersham, making Alaska a territory. Although many Alaskans insisted they deserved to be a full-fledged state, it wasn't until the 1940s that the U.S. government began to seriously consider its statehood.

During World War II, the Defense Department constructed military bases and the Alaska Highway. When the Japanese bombed Dutch Harbor and occupied Attu and Kiska islands in 1942, the strategic military importance of Alaska was apparent. After the war, many military people remained in the territory, but adversaries of statehood argued that its population was still too sparse and its location too distant for it to be a state.

Another argument against statehood was Alaska's lack of a sound economic base. The discovery of oil in 1957 helped the territory leap the final hurdle toward becoming a state. As Alaska's immense wealth of resources was realized, Congress was quickly convinced to disregard past arguments against statehood. Jan. 3, 1959, President Dwight D. Eisenhower signed into law the 49th state of the union.

See also *Alaska Highway, William A. Egan, Ernest Gruening, Oil, Judge James Wickersham & World War II.*

◆ Georg Wilhelm Steller

Georg Wilhelm Steller sailed with Vitus Bering in 1741. The famous German naturalist sketched many plants and animals during the voyage. Today, an eider, jay and sea lion are named for him.

See also *Vitus Bering & Kayak Island.*

◆ Hudson Stuck

Hudson Stuck (1863-1920), archdeacon of the Alaskan missions of the Episcopal Church, traveled tens of thousands of miles throughout Alaska by dog sled and boat. He recorded detailed accounts of the landscape and its accompanying Native names. In 1913, Stuck was a member of the first known party to successfully climb Mt. McKinley/Denali.

◆ Subsistence

The term subsistence refers to traditional methods of hunting, gathering and fishing, or, living off the resources of the land and sea. Today, most people in Alaska relying on subsistence methods are also involved in some type of cash employment. The subsistence lifestyle often requires such modern amenities as gasoline, outboard motors, snow machines, rifles and ammunition.

Many Alaska Natives continue to depend on subsistence methods for a livelihood. Families often combine resources, alternating among themselves in wage and subsistence activities. A growing number of non-Natives also try to live off the land in rural Alaska. Special subsistence hunting and fishing regulations apply.

See also *The Bush & Natives.*

◆ Sundog

A sundog is an optical illusion consisting of one or two colorful circles around the sun, sometimes seen on cold winter days. It is caused by the refraction of light on ice crystals in the air.

◆ Taiga

Taiga forests—coniferous forests dominated by spruce and fir—grow in interior Alaska's subarctic region and often are stunted in size. Taiga is a term of Russian origin meaning "land of little sticks," referring to the scant growth of trees.

See also *Timber & Vegetation.*

◆ Talkeetna

Talkeetna (pop. 250), at the junction of the Talkeetna and Susitna rivers, is a major jumping-off point for climbing expeditions to Mt. McKinley/Denali. The town is also popular with big game hunters, river runners and guides. Talkeetna was settled in 1901 in conjunction with nearby coal, gold and silver mines in the Talkeetna Mountains. It reportedly gets its name from an Indian word meaning "where the rivers meet."

See also *Mt. McKinley/Denali & Mountaineering.*

◆ Termination Dust

Termination dust is a term Alaskans use for the first dusting of snow each autumn, signifying the true end of summer and the start of the long winter season.

◆ Timber

Almost one-third of Alaska is covered by forest, and the state ranks second in the United States in the export of forest products. Combined, Alaska's timber, fishing and mining industries represent 6 percent of the gross state product. The Alaska forest products industry consists of the logging, lumber and pulp industries, which process mainly hemlock, spruce and cedar. Timber operations are based in Southeast's coastal rain forest, with centers in Ketchikan and Sitka. The Interior's forests of spruce, birch and aspen also contribute to the industry.

See also *Industry & Vegetation.*

◆ Time Zones

Prior to October 1983, Alaska had four time zones. At the state's request, the federal government reduced this to two. Most of Alaska now operates on Alaska time (one hour earlier than Pacific time). The Aleutian islands of Atka, Adak, Shemya and Attu operate on Aleutian-Hawaii time (one hour earlier than Alaska time).

◆ Tlingit Indians

In southeastern Alaska, most Native villages are Tlingit settlements. (The Haida Indians have a few settlements in the southern panhandle and the Tsimshian Indians live at Metlakatla on Annette Island in Southeast). The Tlingits are fairly recent immigrants from Canada. They've been in Alaska for hundreds of years, not thousands like the Eskimos and Aleuts, but the Tlingits were well-established in Southeast by the time Europeans first landed in North America in the 18th century. With villages scattered from Ketchikan to Katalla, many signs of Southeast's Tlingit heritage are evident, including physical reminders such as totems, and the continuing use of many Native place names.

The Tlingits were renowned for their fierce warriors, especially those of Kake and Angoon. The bountiful land and sea allowed them to spend less time on hunting and fishing and more on developing a complex culture, with involved rituals, fierce disputes, detailed folklore and beautiful artwork.

All Tlingits belonged to one of two phratries, or kinship groups—the Ravens and the Eagles. Each group was also divided into a number of clans, represented by a characteristic animal, such as Wolf, Bear or Coho, that was the individual symbol of the clan. Their history and traditions bear similarities to that of the Haida Indians. Though the languages and cultures of the Tlingits and Haidas differ, both peoples had capitalist, not socialist, societies (the Athabascans, Eskimos and Aleuts all had socialist societies) and they lived off the land and sea of southeastern Alaska. The Tlingits and Haidas had a deep respect for the natural world, which provided them with everything they needed to live.

See also *Admiralty Island, Carving and Sculpture, Chilkat Blankets, Kake, Natives & Totem Poles.*

◆ Tok

Tok (pop. 935), at the junction of the Alaska Highway and the Tok Cutoff of the Glenn Highway, is a major overland point of entry to Alaska. For many summer travelers coming up the Alaska Highway, Tok is their first stop in the state. The town began as a construction camp on the Alaska Highway, and today is a trade and service center for all types of transportation.

See also *Alaska Highway.*

◆ Tokeen

Old Tokeen, 7 miles northwest of the present settlement of Tokeen, once had Alaska's largest marble quarry. All that's left today of the site on Marble Island are piles of waste marble. Between 1905 and 1932, Tokeen marble was used in the Federal Building in Fairbanks, the Capitol Building in Juneau, Washington's state capitol in Olympia, WA, and in various other buildings throughout the nation.

◆ Tongass National Forest

The 16.8-million-acre Tongass National Forest encompasses about 75 percent of all the land in southeastern Alaska. Tongass, the largest national forest in the United States, was created in 1907 by President Theodore Roosevelt, to protect the coastal rain forest, numerous islands and glaciated mountains of Southeast. The name Tongass comes from the Tongass clan of Tlingit Indians who lived on an island at the southern end of the forest.

Since Tongass is managed as a working forest, it allows for logging, mining and recreational activities. The terrain is mostly covered by forests of western hemlock, hemlock, Sitka spruce, red and yellow cedar, red alder, black cottonwood and lodgepole pine; but it varies with areas of muskeg bogs, glacial outwash plains and marshlands. The land is rich in wildlife and the water teems with fish. Dall and harbor porpoises, hair seals, and humpback and killer whales also populate the waters. Recreational activities vary from camping, hiking, fishing and hunting to public-use cabins and berry picking. Tongass National Forest includes 19 wilderness areas and two national monuments (Admiralty Island and Misty Fiords).

For further information contact the Tongass National Forest Regional Office in Juneau (address in For More Information section).

See also *Admiralty Island, Chugach National Forest, Misty Fiords National Monument & Tracy Arm-Fords Terror Wilderness Area.*

◆ Totem Poles

Totem poles, a product of the Tlingit and Haida cultures, are unique to the Northwest Coast of North America. Totem poles were traditionally erected as story poles, depicting the history of a clan; as memorials to a chief, respected individual or deceased elder; or as artistic expressions of wealth and power. The Haida Indians are thought to have carved the first totem poles, an art which developed from the tradition of carving and painting house posts at the entrances of community houses.

Totem poles are usually carved from red or yellow cedar. Pigments made from soil, berry juice and spruce sap were used to paint them in traditional colors of black, white, red and brown. Modern paints added more colors. Prior to the use of steel tools, obtained from traders in the late 1700s, Indians used stone, bone and shell to carve totems. Some totems were more than 60 feet tall. Today, such tall poles are rare; smaller totems are carved.

Just after the turn of the century, many totem poles were neglected or destroyed at the prompting of Christian missionaries, who mistakenly thought they were an idolic, pagan influence. Left to stand, totems usually decay and fall after about 50 or 60 years.

Visitors may view totem poles at a variety of locations, including Sitka National Historical Park; Totem Bight Park, Saxman Totem Park and the Totem Heritage Cultural Center (in the Ketchikan area); and Klawock Totem Park on Prince of Wales Island.

See also *Carving and Sculpture, Haida Indians, Ketchikan, Sitka National Historical Park & Tlingit Indians.*

✦ Tourism

The first tourists steamed to Alaska in 1884, but the modern tourism industry began after World War II, with the opening of the Alaska Highway in 1948 and the Alaska Marine Highway System in 1963. Tourists are drawn by the amazing diversity of the 49th state, with its glaciers, wildlife, Native arts and culture, historic mining towns, Russian heritage, national parks and monuments, outdoor recreation and museums. Seventy percent of tourists visit during the summer months, with 40 percent coming from the West Coast of the United States. The annual number of tourists has grown to about 900,000 a year.

Alaska's 10 most-visited attractions are:

- Portage Glacier
- The Inside Passage
- Mendenhall Glacier
- Glacier Bay
- The Ketchikan Totems
- Mt. McKinley/Denali
- Skagway's Historic District
- The Anchorage Museum of Art and History
- The University of Alaska Museum
- The Kenai River

For further information on visiting Alaska consult *The MILEPOST®*, the bible of North Country travel since 1949, and *The ALASKA WILDERNESS GUIDE*, both available from Vernon Publications. Visitors can also contact the Alaska Division of Tourism. (Addresses and phone numbers in For More Information section.)

See also *Alaska Highway, Alaska Marine Highway, Glacier Bay National Park, Inside Passage, Kenai Peninsula, Ketchikan, Mendenhall Glacier, Mt. McKinley/Denali, Museums, Portage Glacier & Skagway.*

✦ Tracy Arm-Fords Terror Wilderness Area

Fords Terror earned its name in 1889 when a crew member of a navy vessel rowed into the narrow canyon at low tide. He was caught in the turbulent, iceberg-laden currents for six "terrifying" hours while the tide changed.

The highlights of the Tracy Arm-Fords Terror Wilderness Area are Tracy and Endicott arms. They are long, deep and narrow fjords that extend more than 30 miles into the heavily glaciated Coast Mountain Range. Tidewater glaciers continually calve icebergs at the head of both fjords and wildlife abounds, including eagles, bears, mountain goats, wolves and otters. Area boat tours are a popular tourist attraction. The 653,179-acre wilderness area is located within Tongass National Forest. For further information consult *The ALASKA WILDERNESS GUIDE* (Vernon Publications Inc.) or Juneau Visitor Information (addresses and phone numbers in For More Information section).

See also *Tongass National Forest.*

◆ Trans-Alaska Pipeline

In 1968, the Atlantic Richfield Co. discovered vast amounts of oil at Prudhoe Bay in the Arctic Ocean, which prompted immediate research to determine the best way to transport oil to the Lower 48. An ice-breaking tanker, the Manhattan, was sent to the Arctic Ocean in 1969, but the thick ice damaged the tanker's hull, convincing the oil companies that an overland pipeline was a more feasible solution.

The overland route had its opponents. Environmentalists and Alaska Natives halted its development by filing lawsuits that claimed a pipeline would destroy land that had been occupied by Natives for generations and was rightfully theirs. With pressure from large oil companies to resolve the issue quickly, an agreement was reached in 1971 between Alaska Natives and the federal government with the Alaska Native Claims Settlement Act.

After the land issue was resolved, a variety of engineering problems had to be met. From Prudhoe Bay to Valdez, the ice-free port on Prince

William Sound that was chosen to be the terminus, the pipeline would have to cross three major mountain ranges and the migration paths of caribou and moose. More than half of the line would have to be built on unstable muskeg ground underlain with permafrost. In addition, the line would cross active fault lines, and an all-weather road would have to be constructed from Fairbanks to the North Slope.

By June 20, 1977, the pipeline was completed. It was

Jerrianne Lowther

built by the Alyeska Pipeline Service Co., a consortium of eight oil corporations. Engineers had overcome the problems associated with unstable ground due to permafrost and earthquakes by elevating half of the 800-mile pipeline. The elevated portion is held by 78,000 supports laid out in a zigzag pattern; the design allows the pipeline to move without breaking in the case of an earthquake and holds the hot oil high enough above the permafrost to keep it from thawing the ground and destroying the natural terrain. Hundreds of animal crossings let moose and caribou follow their traditional migration routes.

The first oil took 38 days, 12 hours and 54 minutes to travel through the pipeline, arriving at Valdez on July 28. The pipeline crosses the Brooks, Alaska and Chugach mountains. Prudhoe Bay is now accessible by the Dalton Highway, also known as the North Slope Haul Road, built to transport workers, equipment and machinery from Fairbanks. The total cost of the pipeline and related projects, including the tanker terminal at Valdez, 12 pumping stations and the Yukon River bridge, was $8 billion.

See also *Alaska Native Claims Settlement Act, Coldfoot, Oil & Valdez.*

◆ Tsimshians

In 1887, about 400 Tsimshian Indians left their home near Prince Rupert, BC, and migrated to Annette Island in southeastern Alaska. Rev. William Duncan, a Scottish-born Anglican minister, orchestrated the move after a falling out with church authorities. He encouraged the tribe to start anew on reservation land given to them by the U.S. government.

The Tsimshians built a modern village, called Metlakatla, and commercial fishing has provided most of their income. Metlakatla (pop. 1,407) also has a salmon cannery, fish traps and timber industry jobs. Annette Island retains the status of a federal Indian reservation; since the enactment of the Alaska Native Claims Settlement Act in 1971, it is the only reservation land in the state.

See also *Alaska Native Claims Settlement Act, Haida Indians, Natives & Tlingit Indians.*

◆ Tundra

Almost one-third of Alaska land is tundra, treeless terrain underlain with permafrost. Tundra supports low-growth vegetation such as lichen, mosses, shrubs and flowering plants. The frozen subsoil keeps plants from developing deep roots, stunting any tall growth. Precipitation may be as low as the desert-like level of 5 inches per year; however, the ground is often damp because permafrost and low temperatures prevent evaporation and absorption of moisture. During summer, the marshy land supports a thick population of mosquitoes.

See also *Insects, Lichen, Muskeg & Permafrost.*

◆ The Tundra Times

The first statewide newspaper devoted principally to Native issues, the *Tundra Times* began publishing in 1962. Howard Rock, an Inupiat artist and spokesman, was the editor. An influential and respected writer, Rock was also involved in the drafting of the Alaska Native Claims Settlement Act. He died in 1976, but the *Tundra Times* continues to be published by the Eskimo, Indian, Aleut Publishing Co. in Anchorage.

See also *Alaska Native Claims Settlement Act, Eskimos & Natives.*

◆ Turnagain Arm

Turnagain Arm, a 48-mile estuary leading from the head of Cook Inlet to the mouth of the Placer River, was named by Capt. James Cook on June 1, 1778. Cook was in search of the Northwest Passage, a route from the Pacific to the Atlantic Ocean, when he traveled to the end of the estuary and was unable to proceed any further. Cook, frustrated at hitting another dead end in his search for the passage, named the arm "Turnagain."

Turnagain Arm has a striking landscape. Extensive mud flats are exposed at low tides and accumulated glacial sediment is churned over each time the tide changes. The mud flats themselves are treacherous. The glacial silt and water can create a dangerous quicksand that has trapped the unwary.

The 1964 Good Friday Earthquake caused the land where the town of Portage stood to fall 6 to 11 feet. The resulting flood of salt water into area groundwater killed many trees. Their remains and the remains of abandoned houses may be seen from the Seward Highway.

See also *Captain James Cook, Good Friday Earthquake & Northwest Passage.*

◆ Tussocks and Hummocks

A tussock is a patch of solid ground in boggy or marshy land, held together by dense grasses or roots. A hummock is a ridge, mound or hill, which is often made of snow or ice.

◆ Tyonek

In 1965, the Tyonek Indians won a landmark decision when a federal court ruled that the Bureau of Indian Affairs had no right to lease Tyonek Reservation land for oil development without permission of the Indians. The tribe subsequently sold the rights to drill for oil and gas beneath reservation land to a group of oil companies. They invested the $12.9 million earnings for the benefit of Tyonek residents, most of whom continue to follow a subsistence lifestyle of fishing, hunting and trapping.

U

◆ Ulu

The ulu, or Eskimo woman's knife, is an all-purpose, traditional tool used for cutting and scraping. An ulu has a flat, fan-shaped blade with a center grip. In recent years it has become a popular and useful souvenir.

◆ Umiak

Umiaks—open, skin-covered boats—have been used for hundreds of years by Eskimos in the Bering and Chukchi seas to hunt whales, seals and walrus. The resilient skin shell of the traditional umiak withstands contact with sea ice, and its light weight allows it to be easily carried by two men. An umiak is normally 35 to 40 feet in length and is made of walrus or seal skin stretched over a wooden frame. Although umiaks must be dried regularly to keep the skin from decaying, umiaks are more easily cared for than wooden boats, requiring no varnishing or refinishing.

Frank Whaley Photo

◆ Unalakleet

In Unalakleet (pronounced YOU-na-la-kleet) on the eastern shore of Norton Sound, archeologists have dated house pits along an old beach ridge at 200 B.C. to 300 A.D. Because the town (pop. 714) is located at the terminus of a long-used winter trail from Anvik on the Yukon River, the inhabitants are a mixed race of the Eskimo and Athabascan peoples who used the trail. Today, it forms a leg of the Iditarod Trail Sled Dog Race from Anchorage to Nome.

In 1898, reindeer herders from Lapland settled at Unalakleet; some of their descendants still live in the area. Unalakleet's Eskimo name, *Ounakalik*, means "where the east wind blows."

See also *Iditarod Trail Sled Dog Race.*

◆ Unalaska

Unalaska, on the northern end of Unalaska Island (the second island in the Aleutian chain), was the early headquarters of the Russian-American Co. and a key port for the sea otter fur trade in the 1700s. During the Klondike gold rush of 1897-98, the port of Unalaska was opened as a U.S. Customs port, and it became a major stop for ships heading to and from Nome's gold fields in the early part of this century.

In 1939, during World War II, the U.S. Army and Navy began building installations at Dutch Harbor and Unalaska. Dutch Harbor, the major port area, is on Amaknak Island, and is connected by bridge to Unalaska; but in 1942, when Unalaska was incorporated, Dutch Harbor and Amaknak Island were included. The area was bombed by the Japanese in June 1942, and almost all of the local Aleut people were evacuated to southeastern Alaska. The Dutch Harbor Naval Base and Fort Mears on Amaknak Island have since been designated national historic landmarks.

Two other attractions on the National Register of Historic Places are the Russian Orthodox Church of the Holy Ascension in Unalaska (built in 1825) and the Sitka Spruce Plantation in Dutch Harbor, which consists of six trees planted by Russians in 1805 that have survived in the harsh climate of the naturally treeless Aleutians. At the entrance of the airport is a memorial to those killed in the Aleutians during World War II.

Today, Unalaska (pop. 3,089) is a major civilian port and gateway to the Bering Sea region. One of most productive seafood processing ports in the United States, it remains ice-free year-round. Five shore-based processors form the basis for the local economy, handling king and tanner crab, halibut, salmon, cod and surimi. Dutch Harbor ranks first in the United

States for volume of fish landed (736 million pounds in 1992) and value of catch ($194 million).

The climate is affected by the warm Japan Current flowing from the south that meets the colder air and water currents of the Bering Sea. The opposing currents create storm centers that sweep westward, causing tremendous winds and days of almost constant rain. Makushin Volcano, at 6,000 feet, forms the highest peak of the mountainous island. Unalaska's higher elevations remain snow covered for most of the year.

See also *Aleutian Islands & World War II.*

◆ Unimak Island

Unimak Island, the largest island of the eastern Aleutians, is home to the snow-covered volcanoes of Shishaldin, known locally as Smoking Moses, and Pogromni, whose Russian name means "desolation." Shishaldin has erupted several times in recent years. Unimak is the first of the Aleutian chain, separated from the mainland by narrow Isanotski Strait, also known as False Pass. Capt. Cook recorded the island's Aleut name in 1778, spelling it "Oonimak."

See also *Aleutian Islands & Volcanoes.*

◆ Unga Island Petrified Forest

On Unga Island in the Aleutian chain, black, yellow and gray petrified stumps measuring two to four feet in diameter cover 150 acres of beach. Although the Aleutians are one of the most extensive treeless zones in the world, Unga's petrified forest and petrified wood on Amchitka and Atka islands indicate that the area once supported ancestors of the redwood tree. Eleven to 25 million years ago, during the Miocene period, warmer temperatures allowed metasquoia trees to survive on the stormy, windswept Aleutians.

See also *Aleutian Islands & Vegetation.*

◆ Universities and Colleges

The University of Alaska, a Land and Sea Grant institution, was established in 1917 by Alaska's territorial legislature as the Alaska Agricultural College and School of Mines. In 1935, it was named the University of Alaska. Its multi-campus universities of Fairbanks, Anchorage and Southeast (Juneau) serve a broad array of students. The university is particularly committed to providing educational opportunities for Alaska's Native and rural populations. Enrollment at the three campuses has exceeded 30,000 students in recent years.

Alaska also has five private colleges and universities: Alaska Pacific University (formerly Alaska Methodist University) in Anchorage, Sheldon Jackson College in Sitka, Alaska Bible College in Glennallen and Alaska Business College in Anchorage.

◆ Valdez

Valdez (pop. 4,068), on Prince William Sound, was established in 1897 as a port of entry for gold-seekers bound for the Klondike goldfields. Miners rested and bought supplies before heading north. The Valdez trail to the Klondike was an especially deadly route, with the first part of it leading over Valdez Glacier, where early stampeders faced dangerous crevasses, snowblindness and exhaustion.

In the early 1900s, copper discoveries in the Wrangell Mountains north of Valdez brought more development. The U.S. Army developed the old gold rush trail out of Valdez into a sled and wagon road, routed through Thompson Pass (rather than over Valdez Glacier). The Alaska Road Commission further developed the wagon road, building an automobile road from Valdez to Fairbanks, which was completed in the early 1920s. During World War II, Valdez was linked to the Alaska Highway via the Richardson Highway.

In 1964, the Good Friday earthquake, the most destructive quake ever to hit the southcentral region, virtually destroyed Valdez. A seismic tidal wave washed over the Valdez wharf and engulfed the downtown area. By late August 1964, work was under way to relocate Valdez on more stable ground to the west. The old townsite is located four miles east of present day Valdez, closer to Valdez Glacier.

Another major event that helped shape the face of Valdez was the discovery of oil at Prudhoe Bay in 1968. Port Valdez, the most northerly ice-free port in the Western Hemisphere, was chosen as the pipeline terminus for the multi-billion-dollar project that would transport oil from the North Slope to tankers in Prince William Sound. Construction of the trans-Alaska pipeline, which began in 1974 and was completed in 1977, brought thousands of workers and their families to Valdez. The marine terminal of the Alyeska pipeline is across the bay from the city of Valdez.

See also *Alaska Syndicate, Gold, Minerals, Oil, Prince William Sound & Trans-Alaska Pipeline.*

◆ Valley of Ten Thousand Smokes

See *Katmai National Monument.*

◆ Vegetation

Altogether, 1,500 species of plants grow in Alaska. About half of Alaska is covered with tundra vegetation, which consists mainly of lichens, mosses, sedges and flowering plants. Wildflowers on the tundra include aster, fireweed, forget-me-not, larkspur and laurel. In the mountains, arctic daisies, cowslips, violets and wild hyacinths bloom.

Almost one-third of the state is forested, although northern and western Alaska, the Alaska Peninsula and the Aleutian Islands are virtually treeless. In Southeast and Southcentral, thick forests are composed mainly of Sitka spruce and hemlock. The Interior has stands of black and white spruce, birch and aspen.

See also *Berries, Devil's Club, Fireweed, Lichen, State Symbols, Taiga, Timber, Tundra & Unga Island Petrified Forest.*

◆ Volcanoes

On average, one volcano erupts each year in Alaska. Usually the eruptions are of ash, not lava (as in Hawaii). Most of Alaska's volcanoes are in the Aleutian Islands and on the Alaska Peninsula, which form part of the "ring of fire" that edges the Pacific Ocean.

One of the most powerful eruptions in modern times was the 1912 eruption at Novarupta Volcano, near Mt. Katmai, which blew more than 6 cubic miles of ash and pumice. In 1989-90, Redoubt Volcano had the second most costly volcanic eruption in U.S. history (only the 1980 eruption of Mt. St. Helens in Washington state was costlier). Redoubt was declared dormant in spring 1991. In 1976, Augustine Volcano in the Cook Inlet region—which has erupted seven times since 1812—spewed ash over a

100,000-square-mile area. Other recent eruptions include Mt. Veniaminov in 1984 and Mt. Spurr in 1992. In addition, Mounts Pavlov and Shishaldin have both erupted more than 25 times in the past 200 years.

The five tallest volcanic peaks are Mt. Wrangell (14,163 feet), Mt. Torbert (11,413), Mt. Spurr (11,069), Redoubt Volcano (10,197) and Iliamna Volcano (10,016).

See also *Aniakchak National Monument and Preserve, Katmai National Park and Preserve & Unimak Island.*

♦ Wainwright

Wainwright (pop. 492), on the Chukchi Sea coast, is the largest northern settlement between Barrow and Point Hope. For centuries, villages have stood on this spot of land between Wainwright Inlet (from which the town gets its name) and the sea. The spring whale hunt continues to be a major event for this Eskimo village, providing an important food source for residents. Wainwright Inlet was named in 1826 by British Capt. F.W. Beechey for his officer, Lt. John Wainwright.

See also *Eskimos, Umiak & Whaling*.

♦ Wales

Wales (pop. 161), an Eskimo village, is located on the western tip of the Seward Peninsula on the coast of Cape Prince of Wales—the westernmost point of mainland Alaska. Cape Mountain (2,289 feet), which rises above Wales, is the terminus of the Continental Divide, which separates the Arctic and Pacific watersheds.

Archeological evidence, including a burial mound of the Birnirk culture (500 A.D. to 900 A.D.) discovered behind Wales, indicates the area has been inhabited for centuries. Several prosperous, coastal villages were discovered on Cape Prince of Wales in the early 1800s; however, the Eskimo population was decimated during the worldwide influenza epidemic of 1918-19. Present-day residents of Wales continue to live a traditional lifestyle of hunting, fishing and trapping. In addition, they do some mining and sell Native arts and crafts.

◆ Walrus

Pacific walrus migrate annually between the Chukchi and Bering seas in Alaska. Walrus feed on invertebrates, such as clams, snails and shrimp, and may also hunt seals. A bull walrus can weigh up to 2 tons and reach 12 feet in length.

The Alaska walrus population reached a low in the 1930s, when a downturn in whaling led many whalers to hunt walrus instead. Since then, populations have increased because of protective laws.

The walrus is prized by Natives, who hunt it for food, and also for its ivory tusks and its skin. Walrus ivory is used in carving. Walrus skin is used for making boats; the intestines are made into raincoats.

See also *Ivory, Umiak & Whaling.*

◆ Wasilla

One of the Matanuska–Susitna Valley's pioneer communities, Wasilla (pop. 4,714) began as an Alaska Railroad station in 1916. Located on the George Parks Highway, about 40 miles from Anchorage, Wasilla, is the largest community between Anchorage and Fairbanks, and is a service center for the Matanuska–Susitna Valley.

◆ Weasels

In Alaska, the weasel family is represented by the marten, mink, ermine, least weasel, wolverine and otter. The ermine (or short-tailed weasel) and the least weasel are too small to play an important role in the fur trade. The marten and mink, however, are highly valued for their furs. Marten (also called American sable) have a sharp face, long and bushy tail, and weigh 2 to 3 pounds; their fur is brown with a yellowish or orange area at the throat and neck. Mink are dark brown with a white chin. They have a long body and neck and weigh 2 to 4 pounds.

The wolverine has glossy brown fur, marked on each side with a lighter-colored stripe. They have a gray face with a black muzzle, a bushy tail and long, curved claws. The largest land-dweller of the weasel family (sea otters are larger), wolverines weigh up to 35 pounds.

See also *Otters.*

◆ Whales

Fifteen species of whales are found in Alaska waters: blue, fin, right, bowhead, sperm, sei, gray, humpback, giant bottlenose, goose-beaked, Bering Sea beaked, minke, killer (orca), beluga and narwhal. Most of these species migrate to Alaska during the summer months, spending the rest of the year in the warmer waters of Hawaii and Mexico. A few species reside permanently in Alaska waters, including the beluga, bowhead and narwhal, which live in the Arctic Ocean. Whales can be divided into two categories: baleen whales, which feed on fish and krill filtered from sea water; and toothed whales, which hunt other marine mammals, like the seal and porpoise.

The blue whale, a baleen whale that inhabits the Bering, Chukchi and Beaufort seas from June to October, migrates close to shore, making it the best studied of the whale species.

The humpback is the most acrobatic of the whale family, heaving out of the water in an action known as breaching. Summer visitors to Southeast, Southcentral and Southwest Alaska may see these baleen whales, with their distinctive large flippers and humped backs, breaching offshore or near tour boats. Prince William Sound and Glacier Bay are important summer feeding grounds for humpbacks.

The killer whale, or orca, with its distinctive black and white markings, is also a commonly sighted member of the whale family. Orcas come in resident pods, feeding on fish (mostly salmon), and in transient pods that hunt other marine mammals, including other whales. Their name is thought to come from whalers who called them "whale killer," which became killer whale.

Narwhals inhabit the Arctic Ocean and adjacent seas, but are rare in Alaska waters. The male narwhal has a single, unicorn-like tusk growing from its snout. In old bulls, the tusk may reach 8 feet in length. The function of the tusk has not been established. Narwhals reach about 16 feet in length.

See also *Baleen & Whaling.*

◆ Whaling

For more than 1,000 years, Eskimos of northwestern Alaska have hunted whales; today they represent the only surviving whaling culture in Alaska. The Aleuts were also skilled whalers who developed complex rituals and superstitions based on the hunt. After a man speared a whale, he would seclude himself and even imitate a dying whale, willing the hunt to be successful while other men watched the wounded whale.

Native hunters utilize almost every part of a whale—including its blubber, skin, intestines, baleen and bones—for food, fuel, building materials, tools and artwork. One whale can feed an entire village for months, and in Eskimo communities the spring whaling season is the focal point of the year. The Tlingit and Haida Indians, who live on the coast of southeastern Alaska, are not whale hunters, though in the past they have used beached whales for food and other purposes.

In the late 1700s, Russians began establishing shore-based whaling stations at Kodiak, where they forced Aleut hunters to work for them, and by 1835, Yankee whalers began hunting in Alaska waters. In search of the oil- and baleen-rich bowhead whale, the whalers also hunted sperm, blue, humpback and fin whales. From 1835 until 1871, the owners of whaling fleets made fabulous profits, though the hunters themselves were paid fairly little. In those years, one bowhead whale, yielding 325 barrels of oil and 3,500 pounds of baleen, could be worth $10,000.

But whalers were forced to head further and further north into the Arctic ice pack, as the whales retreated and their numbers declined. Whalers also began hunting walrus by the thousands. The smaller sea mammal yielded far less oil than whales, but its ivory tusks brought additional profits.

1871 proved a disastrous year for whalers and a turning point in the industry. Local Eskimos had predicted to the whalers that an unusually severe winter was encroaching, but their warnings went unheeded. In September, caught by an early winter freeze, 31 New England ships were crushed by the arctic ice pack after repeated attempts to sail out. The Eskimos were aware of the crews' dilemma but were unable to offer housing to the men for the upcoming winter because their main food sources, the whale and walrus, had been decimated. More than 1,000 whalers escaped in 200 small whaling boats, abandoning the large ships and their valuable loads. They were rescued by another fleet of Yankee whalers who were south of the ice pack.

Whalers continued to hunt into the 20th century, but the industry never fully recovered from the 1871 disaster. Today, Alaska's marine mammals are protected by the federal government. It is illegal for anyone other than an Alaska Native to kill a marine mammal.

See also *Alaska Eskimo Whaling Commission, Aleuts, Barrow, Eskimos, Point Hope, Umiak & Whales.*

◆ White Alice

During the 1950s, White Alice was one of two costly defense systems constructed to guard the northern shores of Alaska. The other was the Distant Early Warning (DEW) Line. White Alice, an intricate communications system using twin antennas, was designed to allow radio contact with the most distant Alaska outposts, no matter what the weather conditions. Prior to White Alice, radio communications in northern Alaska would often be incomprehensible or go dead with no warning, due to sunspot activity, atmospheric static or inclement weather.

The project's code name, White Alice, came from the combination of White, for wintertime Alaska, and Alice, for Alaska Integrated Communications Enterprise. Today, satellite communications are used, and the system, state-of-the-art in the 1950s, is obsolete.

See also *DEW Line.*

◆ Whittier

More than half the population of Whittier (pop. 243), at the head of Passage Canal on Prince William Sound, is housed in the 14-story Begich towers, formerly called the Hodge Building. It was renamed for U.S. Rep. Nick Begich of Alaska, who along with Rep. Hale Boggs of Louisiana was killed in a plane crash near Whittier in 1972. (The visitor center at Portage Glacier is also named for the congressmen.)

The rest of the population lives in Whittier Manor, built in the 1950s, and the Buckner Building. The Buckner Building, completed in 1953, was once the largest building in the state—known as the "city under one roof."

The town of Whittier, named after the American poet John Greenleaf Whittier (1807-92), is connected to the Seward Highway by railroad and to other communities by ferry. Whittier was created by the U.S. government during World War II as a port and petroleum delivery center that was tied to bases farther north by the Alaska Railroad and later a pipeline. Whittier became a primary debarkation point for cargo and troops. Construction of the huge buildings that dominate Whittier began in 1948 and the Port of Whittier, strategically valuable for its ice-free deep-water port, was active until 1960.

See also *World War II*.

◆ Judge James Wickersham

In 1900, Judge James Wickersham, from Tacoma, WA, arrived at Eagle as the first judge of the Third Judicial District of Alaska. His district encompassed a 300,000-square-mile area, stretching 2,000 miles from the Arctic Ocean to the Aleutian chain.

Wickersham, an aggressive and ambitious lawyer and politician, had a significant impact on the development of Alaska. At first, he had to contend with a lack of trained lawyers in the district, and with area miners, who preferred their own system of justice—miners' meetings. Wickersham traveled thousands of miles throughout the district by dog sled and steamer. He built a courthouse and a jail in Eagle, but later moved the district seat to the boom town of Fairbanks. (It was Wickersham who suggested the town be named for Indiana Senator Charles W. Fairbanks.)

Wickersham was Alaska's non-voting delegate to U.S. Congress between 1909 and 1917. In 1912, a bill written by Wickersham was passed through Congress giving Alaska territorial status.

See also *Fairbanks*.

◆ Noel Wien

During the pioneering days of Alaskan aviation, Noel Wien was a talented, and already legendary, bush pilot. Wien, who began flying in Alaska in 1924, had an excellent sense of direction; in the worst of weather and despite many forced landings in unfamiliar terrain, Wien never got lost. He pioneered many flight routes between Alaska communities, including the well-traveled Fairbanks-to-Nome route in 1925. He was also the first man to fly north of the Arctic Circle and the first to operate an airline throughout the winter in the Arctic.

In 1927, Wien went into business with his brother Ralph, forming Wien Alaska Airlines, later known also as Wien Consolidated and Wien Air Alaska. Its pilots were sometimes referred to as "Wienie birds." Wien's airline went through a number of mergers in the following years, and was sold to House-

hold Finance Corp. after Wien's death. The airline filed for bankruptcy in 1985, and operated only briefly in 1986. Wien Air Alaska was one of the oldest U.S.-owned airlines and one of the largest employers in Alaska. A helmeted goose was one of its logos.

See also *Aviation, The Bush & Ben Eielson.*

◆ Will Rogers and Wiley Post Monument

In 1935, Will Rogers, the American humorist, and Wiley Post, a famous pilot, were flying to Barrow, a planned stop on their trip from Fairbanks to Siberia. They landed 15 miles south of the community to ask directions; on taking off again, the plane rose 50 feet, stalled and then plunged into a river below, killing both men. Today, the Will Rogers and Wiley Post Monument, dedicated in 1982 to commemorate the two men, stands across from the Barrow airport. Another monument, on the National Register of Historic Places, is located outside of Barrow at the crash site.

◆ Williwaw

A williwaw, or sudden, cold gust of wind, is a common occurrence in the Aleutian Islands, where squalls are created along the mountainous coastline.

See also ***Aleutian Islands.***

◆ Willow

In 1976, Willow (pop. 285), a small town on the George Parks Highway north of Anchorage, was selected to replace Juneau as the capital of Alaska. Since statehood, a number of Alaskans had felt Juneau was a poor site for the capital, as it is hundreds of miles from the population centers of Anchorage and Fairbanks and only accessible by air or water.

After the Alaskan citizens voted to have the capital moved, the government had one committee narrow down a list of possible sites, and then later went so far as to have architects draw up a full plan for a city of more than 30,000 people at the Willow townsite. However, in November 1982 Alaskan voters vetoed the initiative that would have provided funding for the move, and today Willow remains a small stop on the Alaska Railroad.

See also ***Juneau.***

◆ Wolves

Wolves are found throughout Alaska in a variety of terrain. To satisfy their voracious appetites, wolves may consume up to 7 pounds of food per day. They are capable of killing large mammals such as moose and caribou, yet also feed off smaller animals and fish. A wolf's coat may be black, white, gray, brown or yellow.

◆ Wolverines

See *Weasels.*

◆ World Eskimo-Indian Olympics

The World Eskimo-Indian Olympics feature such unique events as the Ear Weight and Ear Pull competitions, the One-Hand Reach, the Four-Man Carry and the Greased Pole Walk. The Olympics have been a success every year since their inception in 1961. Organized as a showcase for Alaska Native athletic games, cultural events, dances and art, the event, held in

Fairbanks each July, has grown to include 25 events and involves visitors from Canada, Russia, Europe and the Lower 48.

The events are designed to demonstrate mental, physical and spiritual strength, and traditional Native skills, such as seal skinning and fish cutting. The Nalukatak (Blanket Toss), the White Men vs. Native Women Tug of War, the Alaskan High Kick, the Knuckle Hop and the One- and Two-Foot High Kicks are popular competitions.

◆ World War II

In June 1942, the Japanese bombed Dutch Harbor and occupied Attu and Kiska islands in the Aleutian chain. Construction of the Alaska Highway, which had begun in April 1942, four months after the United States entered the war, was rushed to completion by October. Thousands of troops were transported to the territory. Under the command of General Simon B. Buckner, secret air bases had been built at Cold Bay in 1941 and on Umnak Island in 1942. In May 1943, Attu and Kiska were retaken. The Aleutian campaign was continuously hampered by the region's terrible weather, including 120-mph winds, fog and constant storms.

During the war years (1939–45), the Territory of Alaska remained under the jurisdiction of the Department of the Interior but was designated a military combat area, and all civilian traffic to, within and from Alaska was controlled by the military's Alaska Travel Control.

See also *Alaska Highway, Aleutian Islands, Attu Island, DEW Line, Kiska Island, Military Bases, Statehood, White Alice & Whittier.*

◆ Wrangell

Wrangell (pop. 2,595) is located on Wrangell Island in Southeast Alaska. Wrangell is the only Alaskan city to have existed under 4 nations and 3 flags: Tlingit, Russia, Great Britain and the United States. It served as a supply point for fur traders and gold seekers on the Stikine River.

A port of call for ferries and cruise ships, Wrangell's Tribal House on Shakes Island is listed on the National Register of Historic Places.

◆ Wrangell–St. Elias National Park and Preserve

In the 13-million-acre Wrangell-St. Elias National Park and Preserve, the Wrangell, St. Elias and Chugach mountains converge—a mountain wilderness unrivaled in North America. Together with Canada's Kluane National Park, which backs Wrangell-St. Elias across the border, the two areas comprise the largest parkland on the continent. Wrangell-St. Elias alone is the largest unit in America's national park system. Established in 1980, the park and preserve contain the greatest collection of peaks above 16,000 feet and the largest concentration of glaciers in North America. Mount St. Elias, at 18,008 feet, is the second-highest peak in the United States.

The spectacular scenery includes the Chitistone and Nizina canyons; the dormant volcanoes of Mt. Blackburn (16,390 feet), Mt. Sanford (16,237) and Mt. Drum (12,010); the active Mt. Wrangell (14,163), which last erupted in 1930; and the impressive Malaspina and Hubbard glaciers. Also, the area has many historical and pre-historical sites: ancient Native villages and camps, sites of Russian fur-trading posts and gold rush relics. The varied wildlife includes bison, caribou, Dall sheep, mountain goats, bears, wolves, wolverines and many small, fur-bearing animals. The Copper River, which flows through the park, is a major salmon spawning ground. Popular activities include hunting and fishing, cross-country skiing, rafting and kayaking.

See also *Hubbard Glacier, Malaspina Glacier & National Parklands.*

◆ Yukon River

The Yukon is the longest river in Alaska, flowing 1,400 miles from the Canadian border to the Bering Sea. The river's total length from its source in northwestern British Columbia to the coast is 2,300 miles. The mighty river travels west through Yukon Territory and the heart of interior Alaska, then empties into Norton Sound. Frozen from October to May, the river floods during its spring thaw.

The Yukon was discovered and explored during the first half of the 19th century, and became a major supply route for interior Alaska. Missionaries, fur trappers and prospectors traveled the Yukon by riverboat in summer and by dog sled in winter. Most of the settlements in interior Alaska are situated on the Yukon and its tributaries, which include the Porcupine, Innoko, Koyukuk and Tanana rivers.

The Yukon continues to be important for local shipping, salmon fishing and hydroelectric power.

See also *Gold, Rivers, Yukon-Charley Rivers National Preserve & Yukon-Kuskokwim Delta.*

◆ Yukon-Charley Rivers National Preserve

The Yukon-Charley Rivers National Preserve contains 128 miles of the historic Yukon River and the entire 106-mile Charley River basin. Along the banks of the broad, swift and silty Yukon remains the 1930s-era Coal Creek mining camp, which includes a large placer gold dredge and various support buildings. But the area supported people long be-fore the arrival of modern-day fortune-seekers. Archeological evidence indicates that much of the area was unglaciated during the last ice age and people have been present for at least 10,000 years.

Originally a national monument, the area was designated a 2.5-million-acre preserve in 1980. The peregrine falcon, an endangered species, nests in the bluffs above the Yukon. More than 200 other bird species have been sighted in the preserve, including bald and golden eagles and gyrfalcons. Moose, lynx, beavers, bears, caribou, wolves and wolverines inhabit the area, too. Common activities include hiking, fishing, dog sledding, snowmobiling, snowshoeing and river floating.

See also *Gold, National Parklands & Yukon River.*

• Yukon-Kuskokwim Delta

For thousands of years, the 2,300-mile-long Yukon River and the 700-mile-long Kuskokwim River have deposited tons of glacial silt into the Bering Sea on Alaska's west coast. The silt has formed one of the largest coastal flood plains in the world—the Yukon-Kuskokwim Delta. In the United States, the vast alluvial plain is exceeded in size only by the Mississippi River delta. The Yukon-Kuskokwim Delta stretches 250 miles along the coast from Kuskokwim Bay to Norton Sound and extends inland 200 miles to the Kuskokwim Mountains.

Most of the delta's terrain is marshy tundra, which makes travel and construction difficult. The landscape is dominated by grays and greens, with frequently cloudy skies and strong winds. About half the land is covered by lakes, streams, sloughs and ponds, making it an excellent wetland breeding ground for waterfowl. The nation's largest wildlife refuge—the Yukon Delta National Wildlife Refuge—encompasses 19.6 million acres of the delta.

More than 100 Native villages are located on the Yukon-Kuskokwim Delta; most are Yup'ik Eskimo, though some Athabascan Indians inhabit the inland portion of the region. Bethel, on the Kuskokwim River, is the commercial and administrative heart of the plain.

See also *Bethel, National Wildlife Refuges & Rivers.*

◆ Russian John Zarnowsky

In 1896, Russian John Zarnowsky unknowingly sold half of the richest gold claim on the richest gold creek in the Far North for a sack of flour and a side of bacon.

His claim was staked just across the Alaska border in Yukon Territory, along a small trickle of stream called "Bonanza's pup" (because of its proximity to the larger Bonanza Creek, already known to be home to magnificent gold deposits). Zarnowsky and other miners had staked claims in the area shortly after George Washington Carmack struck it rich at Bonanza (formerly Rabbit) Creek, but, believing they had already missed out on the big placer deposits in the region, most gambled away or sold their undeveloped claims for a pittance.

Little did they know that "Bonanza's pup" would go down as Eldorado Creek, the most valuable placer discovery in history. "Big Alex" McDonald, the Nova Scotian who bought Russian John Zarnowsky's claim (among others), made a fortune and earned the regional title "The King of the Klondike."

In fact, the discoveries on Eldorado and Bonanza creeks prompted the largest gold stampede of all time—the Klondike gold rush of 1897-98, which left a deep impression on the history of Alaska.

See also *Chilkoot Pass, Gold, Klondike Gold Rush National Historical Park & Skagway.*

FOR MORE INFORMATION

Alaska Aviation Heritage Museum
4721 Aircraft Drive
Anchorage, AK 99502
907-248-5325

Alaska Campground Owner's Association
P.O. Box 84884
Fairbanks, AK 99708
907-883-5877

Alaska Department of Fish and Game
P.O. Box 25526
Juneau, AK 99802-5526
907-465-4180
www.state.ak.us/local/akpages/
FISH.GAME.adfghome.htm

Alaska Division of Tourism
Dept. 201
P.O. Box 110801
Juneau, AK 99811-0801
907-465-2010

Alaska Dog Mushers Association
P.O. Box 70662
Fairbanks, AK 99707-0662
907-457-6874

Alaska Marine Highway System
P.O. Box 25535
Juneau, AK 99802-5535
800-642-0066
www.dot.state.ak.us/external/
amha/home.html

Alaska Public Lands Information Center
605 W. Fourth Avenue, #105
Anchorage, AK 99501-5162
907-271-5555

Alaska Railroad Corp.
Passenger Service Department
P.O. Box 107500
Anchorage, AK 99510-7500
800-544-0552
907-265-2494

Alaska State Parks
Division of Natural Resources
Division of Parks and Outdoor Recreation
3601 C Street, Suite 1200
Anchorage, AK 99503-5921
907-269-8740
www.dnr.state.ak.us

Anchorage Audubon Society
P.O. Box 101161
Anchorage, AK 99510
907-278-3007

Anchorage Convention and Visitors Bureau
524 W. Fourth Avenue
Anchorage, AK 99501
907-274-3531
www.alaska.net/-acvb

Anchorage Museum of History and Art
121 W. Seventh Avenue
Anchorage, AK 99501
907-343-4326

Anchorage Visitor Information Center
Fourth Avenue and F Street
Anchorage, AK 99501
907-274-3531

Bureau of Land Management
1150 University Avenue
Fairbanks, AK 99709-3899
907-474-2251

Chugach National Forest
3301 C Street, Suite 300
Anchorage, AK 99503
907-271-2500

Denali National Park
P.O. Box 9
McKinley Park, AK 99755
907-683-2294
www.nps.gov

**Division of Geological &
Geophysical Survey**
Publications Section
794 University Avenue, Suite 200
Fairbanks, AK 99709-3545
907-451-5000

**Fairbanks Convention and
Visitors Bureau**
550 First Avenue
Fairbanks, AK 99701-4790
800-327-5774
907-456-5774
E-mail: fcvb@polarnet.com

**Forest Service Information
Center**
Centennial Hall
101 Egan Drive
Juneau, AK 99801
907-586-8751

Iditarod Trail Committee
P.O. Box 870800
Wasilla, AK 99687-0800
907-376-5155
www.iditarod.com

Juneau Visitor Information
Davis Log Cabin
134 Third Street
Juneau, AK 99801
907-586-2201

**Ketchikan Convention and
Visitors Bureau**
131 Front Street
Ketchikan, AK 99901-6413
907-225-6166

**Sitka Convention and Visitors
Bureau**
P.O. Box 1226
Sitka, AK 99835
907-747-5940

**Skagway Convention and
Visitors Bureau**
P.O. Box 415
Skagway, AK 99840-0415
907-983-2854

Tongass National Forest
USDA Public Affairs Office
P.O. Box 21628
Juneau, AK 99802-1628
907-271-2737

U.S. Fish and Wildlife Service
1011 E. Tudor Road
Anchorage, AK 99501
907-343-6173

University of Alaska Museum
907 Yukon Drive
Fairbanks, AK 99775
907-474-7505

White Pass & Yukon Route
P.O. Box 435
Skagway, AK 99840
800-343-7373
907-983-2217

From the Editors of Alaska A to Z

The MILEPOST®
49th Edition

'The quintessential reference.'

— The Associated Press

The latest information on everything:
• Cruise ship, ferry, city and highway travel, including the famous Alaska Highway and the beautiful Inside Passage.
• Attractions, activities, recreation, food, gas, camping, lodging, history, scenery, wildlife—everything a traveler needs to know about what to see and do.
• Special features on the Klondike Gold Rush Centennial.
• Detailed four-color maps.
• Hundreds of color photos.
• Completely updated every year.
• Free pullout plan-a-trip map, a $4.95 value!
$21.95, 750-plus pages, softbound.
8 3/8 x 10 7/8 in. ISBN 1-878425-29-3

ALASKA ROADHOUSE RECIPES

'A beautiful book I'll surely keep as a permanent record of our trip.'

— Betty Wilson, Seattle, Wash.

A wonderful souvenir or gift, with recipes from the roadhouses, lodges, bed and breakfasts, cafes, restaurants and campgrounds along the highways and byways of Alaska and Canada. From Copper River King Salmon Chili

and Alaska Rhubarb Pie to Alaska Backpack Mountain Bread and Fiddlehead House Dressing, Alaska Roadhouse Recipes provides a delightful taste of the North Country, with photos and captions profiling personalities and places that contributed to the cookbook.
$16.95, 228 pages, softbound.
8 1/4 x 5 1/4 in. ISBN 1-878425-59-5.

To order, write, phone, fax or e-mail:

Vernon Publications Inc.
3000 Northup Way, Ste. 200 • P.O. Box 96043 • Bellevue, WA 98009-9643
1-800-726-4707 or (425) 827-9900
Fax: (425) 822-9372; E-mail: books@alaskainfo.com

THE ALASKA WILDERNESS GUIDE

7th Edition

'Authoritative guide to the back country.'
— *Anchorage Daily News*

• The single-source book for anyone planning adventure travel in Alaska. Where to go camping, sportfishing, boating, kayaking, river running, hiking and more in Alaska's backcountry, including lodging, services and supplies, and airstrips and seaplane docks.
• Adventure Travel Directory to wilderness lodges, outfitters and bush airlines.
$16.95, 500-plus pages, softbound, 80 photos, color maps and charts. 6 x 9 in. ISBN 1-878425-50-1

Northwest Mileposts®

5th Edition

'One of our favorites. We would have purchased this guidebook purely for its excellent maps, but they are just the tip of the iceberg.'
— *Western RV News*

• The most complete travel guide to Washington, Oregon, Idaho and British Columbia.
• The same mile-by-mile logging style made famous by The MILEPOST®.
• Detailed descriptions of major cities.
• Includes national parks, monuments and recreation areas of the Northwest.

• Detailed color maps. 100-plus color photos.
$16.95, 300-plus pages, softbound.
8 3/8 x 10 7/8 in. ISBN 1-878425-80-3

The MILEPOST® Souvenir Logbook

The perfect companion to The MILE-POST®: A photo book, travel diary, expense record and keepsake all in one — perfect for cruise ship or highway travel. Beautiful color photos, metric conversion table, mileage chart, glossary of Alaska terms and free pullout postcards.
$12.95, 80 pages, Wire-O bound.
5 1/2 x 8 1/4 in. ISBN 1-878425-84-6

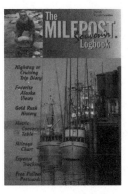

About those vintage photos...

Mac's Foto
Mac's Foto Service in Anchorage (now Alaska Pictorial Service) was—and is—the work of Steve McCutcheon. An award-winning photographer, McCutcheon's Mac's Foto recorded thousands of images of Alaska from the 1940s to present-day.
The photos used in this book appeared in early editions of *The MILE-POST®* and are reprinted here courtesy of Mr. McCutcheon.

Frank Whaley
Frank Whaley ferried a plane to Nome in 1932 and stayed to become the third pilot hired by Wien Alaska Airlines. Also a photographer, he recorded Alaska's people and places throughout his career as a pilot and tour manager for Wien; as one of the founders of the Alaska Visitors Association; and as a territorial senator. Frank Whaley's promotional photos for Wien Alaska Airlines, which appear in these pages, were used in early editions of *The MILEPOST®*. Mr. Whaley has been "thawing out" in Southern California for the last 20 years.

William A. Wallace (Collection)
William A. Wallace published *The MILEPOST®* from 1949 until 1964, and he gathered hundreds of photos during his travels throughout Alaska over the years. The photo collection is archived with Vernon Publications Inc.

"Alaska is the most important place in the world."

 — General Billy Mitchell
